MW00780347

Edgar Cayce on
Mastering Your

Spiritual

Growth

Edgar Cayce on Mastering Your

Spiritual Growth

by Kevin J. Todeschi

Yazdan Publishing • Virginia Beach • Virginia

Selected Books by Kevin J. Todeschi

Dreams, Images and Symbols
Edgar Cayce's ESP
Edgar Cayce on the Akashic Records
Edgar Cayce on Mastering Your Spiritual Growth
Edgar Cayce on Reincarnation and Family Karma
Edgar Cayce on Soul Mates
Edgar Cayce on the Book of Revelation
Edgar Cayce's Twelve Lessons in Personal Spirituality
God In Real Life

Fiction

A Persian Tale
The Reincarnation of Clara
The Rest of the Noah Story

To Joe and Carol,
In love and appreciation for allowing me to discover
that truth is a growing thing.

Copyright © 2011
by Kevin J. Todeschi

Printed in the U.S.A.

All rights reserved. No part of this book may be used or reproduced in any manner whatsoever without written permission except in the case of brief quotations embodied in critical articles of reviews.

Published by:
Yazdan Publishing
P.O. Box 4604
Virginia Beach, VA 23454

[Previously published by A.R.E. Press as *Edgar Cayce on Soul Growth*]

ISBN-13: 978-0-9845672-5-6

Cover design by Richard Boyle
Text and design layout by Cathy Merchand

Edgar Cayce Readings © 1971, 1993-2007
by the Edgar Cayce Foundation.
All rights reserved.

And again he said, Whereunto shall I liken the kingdom of God?

It is like leaven, which a woman took and hid in three measures of meal, till the whole was leavened.

Luke 13:20-21

Table of Contents

Preface .... *xi*

1 The Edgar Cayce Material and Spiritual Growth 1

2 Spiritual Growth Case Histories 20

3 Spiritual Growth Through Meeting Self 53

4 Spiritual Growth and Personal Loss 74

5 Spiritual Growth Through Life's Experiences 90

6 The Nature of the Human Will 114

7 Keys to Spiritual Growth: Ideals, Attunement,
     and Application 134

8 Light to a Waiting World 164

Conclusion *179*

Preface

"Who am I?" "Why am I here?" "What is the purpose of life?" Throughout the history of the world, questions such as these have driven every generation of humankind in search of meaning. Many have discovered partial answers in religion. Some have encountered personal revelation in philosophy. There are even those who have found clarification of their life's purpose in psychology. Others, however, have spent a lifetime in search of answers to questions that they didn't entirely know how to ask.

In much of religious thought, one's ultimate identity is connected with the soul—that portion of each individual that is believed to experience some form of eternity. Generally, it is thought that, through the evolving process of life, each individual begins to shape the "eternity" which becomes one's destiny. In spite of the fact that some people have always maintained a narrow and exclusive look at the liberation and salvation of the soul, for many interested in spirituality, the purpose of life is much more than simply being "bad" or "good" and then receiving the corresponding punishment or reward. For example, in Hinduism there is the belief that, eventually, within each individual, the desire arises to discover an understanding of Brahma, the Creator. Although every soul is a part of Brahma, it is only as the soul ponders and experiences the knowledge of Brahma, the Supreme Universal Soul, that the individual soul gradually begins to awaken to its true selfhood. In time, the soul begins to discover the same powers and attributes within itself that belong to the Creator. The result is that the soul is released from limitation and bondage and truly becomes at one with Brahma, the Whole.

This same idea—that we are somehow integrally connected to the Divine and are destined to become like our Creator—is found in legends, myths, and stories such as the Buddhist parable of the wealthy man and his poor son, contained in the *Lotus Sutra*. In the parable, a young man, apparently in search of himself, leaves his wealthy father's home and roams the country for more than fifty years. Through the course of events, the son experiences extreme poverty and must take on meager jobs simply to pay for his next meal. During those years, the father grows old and moves to an even larger estate, still constantly grieving over the loss of his son.

Eventually, the poor son passes by the gates of a magnificent estate. Peering inside, he can see servants taking care of an old, wealthy gentleman. Unfortunately, because the son has so lost himself, he does not recognize the man as his own father. In spite of the passage of fifty years, however, the father immediately recognizes him and sends well-dressed servants to rescue his now-grown son. Because the son does not recognize his own father, when the servants come to retrieve him, he panics and thinks he is being arrested for a crime he did not commit. It is clear that the son has forgotten his true identity. Not wanting to scare his offspring any further, the father releases his son. A plan is devised through which the son can remember his worth and grow into his inheritance.

Two of the wealthy man's servants dress in shabby clothes and follow after the son to offer him a lowly job on the estate, gathering sewage to make fertilizer, which the son accepts. For twenty years, the son works at this job and begins to gain self-confidence. During that period, the father disguises himself as a foreman and finds occasion to praise his son's efforts. Gradually, the son's faith in himself grows, until the day comes when the foreman offers the son a promotion as an accountant for the entire estate.

Although the son still lacks healthy self-esteem, at the encouragement of the foreman he accepts the position. In time, the son sees how his life has changed, due to his own efforts, from one of poverty and shame to one of responsibility and being able to care for himself. As a result, the son finally acquires self-worth and faith in himself. At this point, the father has become so old and near death that the ruse cannot continue. He declares the truth and makes his son heir to the entire estate.

The dynamics of our deep and literal connection to God is also found in Judeo-Christian scripture, beginning with Genesis, where we are told that God made humankind in the Creator's image. From this perspective, the body is simply an external wrapping for the soul. Interestingly enough, a New Testament version of the Buddhist parable also exists in the parable of the prodigal son (Luke 15:11-24), clearly illustrating the journey of the soul and our connection to God. Simply stated, we were with God in the beginning; through the power of our free will, we were able to make choices that were not necessarily in perfect accord with the Creator, enabling us to forget our true identity. However, at some point, we will "arise" and decide to return to God, regaining our inheritance and finally experiencing our rightful relationship with Him.

In discussing the nature of humankind, American philosopher and editor Paul Carus (1852-1919) often sought the interwoven connections among science, philosophy, and religion. In the preface to his book, *The Soul of Man,* he stated:

> What is more interesting to man than his own soul! And what, at the same time is so mysterious, so wonderful, so marvelous! Our pleasures and pains, our loves and hatreds, our hopes and fears, our longings, our aspirations and ideals, whence do they come, what is their meaning and whither do they tend?
>
> For every one the centre of the universe lies in himself. In our soul, if anywhere, must be sought the key to the mysteries of the cosmos.

This same idea that the discovery of one's purposefulness is ultimately an inward journey is echoed in esoteric and New Thought traditions which state that, although the Divine is everywhere, it isn't until the search leads within one's own self that God can ever really be found.

In exploring the nature of humankind, Carl Gustav Jung (1875-1961), founder of the analytical school of psychology, believed that the goal of personal development was self-realization or individuation. From this premise, the archetype or universal model of every individual's potential was clearly expressed in the Christ. Jung called the Christ "the archetype of the self," for the Christ-figure exemplified the self fully realized: "He represents a totality of a divine or heavenly kind, a glorified man, a son of God . . . unspotted by sin." (*Collected Works,* 9ii) Rather than being a message restricted to a specific religion, from a psychological perspective the Christ embodies a universal archetype of the self for all of humankind. The universality of the Christ is also explored in the work of Edgar Cayce (1877-1945), twentieth-century mystic and clairvoyant. Although Cayce himself was a Christian, his life's work is deeply ecumenical. From Cayce's perspective, regardless of an individual's religious or personal beliefs, the Christ pattern exists in potential upon the very fiber of her or his being. It is that part of each of us that is in perfect accord with the Creator and is simply waiting to find expression in our lives through the use of the will. This Christ pattern was further described as " . . . the awareness within each soul, imprinted in pattern on the mind and waiting to be awakened by the will, of the soul's oneness with God" (5749-14[1]); its manifestation is the eventual destiny of each and every soul. With this in mind, Cayce presented Jesus as humankind's "elder brother," a soul who came to show each one of us the way back to our spiritual Source by perfectly manifesting the laws of the Creator in the earth.

While exploring the philosophical meaning of life, many individuals have incorrectly assumed that the goal of being in the earth is simply to reach heaven, find enlightenment, or somehow "get out of the earth." This is a perspective quite different from that contained in the Cayce material, however. In part, Cayce believed that, as children of God, our mission is to somehow bring *spirit* into the earth, experiencing soul growth and

---

[1]During Cayce's life, the Edgar Cayce readings were all numbered to provide confidentiality. The first set of numbers (e.g., "5749") refers to the individual or group for whom the reading was given. The second set of numbers (e.g., "14") refers to the number in the series from which the reading is taken. For example, 5749-14 identifies the reading as the fourteenth one given to the subject assigned number 5749.

personal development in the process.

Throughout his adult life, Edgar Cayce gave intuitive consultations, called "readings," to individuals from all segments of society and various religious backgrounds. In addition to his work with hundreds of topics, including health and personal counsel, in nearly 2,000 "life readings" Cayce explored for individuals their soul history and their corresponding development through a series of lifetimes. From a source of information he called the "akashic records," Cayce could view an individual's soul development and describe how past-life influences and choices played out over time. Rather than being simply a philosophical discussion of possible past lives and corresponding strengths and weaknesses, the readings detail practical advice regarding what an individual might accomplish in the present, based upon the experiences and influences affecting her or him from the past.

The readings on reincarnation were given to individuals to help them understand soul strengths and weaknesses, as well as their own potentials and challenges. Often, when viewing an individual's soul history, Cayce commented on how the person had both "gained" and "lost" in terms of soul development in any given lifetime. For example, a fifty-three-year-old housewife was told that, in the present, she possessed innate talents as a teacher and a guide to others. Apparently because of past-life experiences, she had developed the ability to attune herself to the Divine, and she could share that same ability with others for their own personal development. Cayce perceived how some of her strengths and weaknesses had been acquired during an incarnation in Greece when she had lived at the time of Xenophon, the Athenian general.

While Xenophon was away on one of his military campaigns, the woman had found herself in a position that enabled her to provide encouragement and assistance to others. In fact, the Grecian life had been a period when she had truly learned to be of service. At the same time, however, after Xenophon's return and his elevating her to a position of responsibility, the woman apparently misused her newly acquired power for personal aggrandizement and the pursuit of selfishness. In summarizing her lifetime in Greece, Cayce stated: "Gaining and losing through the experience. Gaining for the faith and service rendered many during the trials of that waiting. Losing in the mis-application of the power *gained* by being put in an exalted position." (115-1) In the present, the woman was encouraged to set aside her selfish motives and to focus instead upon cultivating her connection to the Divine and continuing to be of service to others.

The Cayce information stresses the continuity of the soul regardless of an individual's bodily identity in any given lifetime. All experiences, inclinations, desires, abilities, and shortcomings from the past become a part of the soul's memory in the present. As to whether a soul is developed or impaired in any given incarnation depends upon an individual's application and the use of his or her free will. Because past-life influences can be both negative and positive, Cayce repeatedly emphasized the important role played by the human will in each soul's personal development. As a case in point, in 1929, Cayce told a fifty-one-year-old osteopath that the will plays a greater role in a person's development than either heredity or environment. It is essentially the will that determines whether a person evolves, grows, and *overcomes life's challenges* or regresses, fails, and is *overcome by them* (101-1).

Just as in the parable of the poor son, Cayce believed that, because of our focus on the material things in life, much of humankind has forgotten its true birthright as a child of a loving God. From this perspective, the material world is simply a faint reflection of a much greater spiritual reality. In fact, the material world might be likened to a purposeful dream that enables each individual to evolve into an awareness of one's true self through lifetimes of experiences, choices, and interactions with others. Cayce told one person:

> For, will is the factor that makes for growth in the soul's sleep through the earth's experience. For, with the birth of a physical body the soul slumbers; and its dreams are the deeds by which the soul is judged in its associations with its fellow man. 259-8

The Cayce information insists that we are not simply physical bodies; instead, we are spiritual beings who are having a physical experience. Essentially, we are all seekers, seeking our true identity and our relationship to the Whole. From this premise, life is an ongoing adventure of purposeful experiences and relationships, enabling each individual to find the true self.

All too often, we have sought meaning in our lives through all manner of escape, acquisition, addiction, and confusion. The time must come in the history of the world when we finally realize that, throughout our sojourns through space and time, we have simply been seeking our connection to spirit, our connection to the Creative Forces, our connection to God. With that in mind, this book is an attempt to explore what constitutes spiritual growth as well as why a soul may lose ground in a particular incarnation. In the end, I hope that it might make some small contribution to our comprehension of the true nature of humankind and to our collective understanding that we are truly spiritual beings.

Kevin J. Todeschi

The Edgar Cayce Material and Spiritual Growth

Soul development should take precedence over all things.   *3357-2*

What if the purpose of life were not simply to be born into a family, go to school, get a job, acquire material goods, create a family of one's own, grow older, and then eventually die, leaving one's descendants and family members to repeat the very same cycle? What if one's life experiences were not simply random chance; instead, some kind of divine purposefulness stood behind the possibilities of every single day for every single individual? What if we suddenly discovered we were somehow actively responsible for cocreating the substance of our lives? What if we came to realize that our perception of ourselves is extremely limited, for we are, in truth, eternal beings possessing infinitely more than an average of seven to ten decades of life? What if the answer to the question "Who am I?" were much more than we had ever even dared to imagine?

Perhaps more than anything else, humankind is in need of an entire worldview shift—a change in our collective perception that will enable all individuals to look at themselves and one another in a completely new light. This change in perception needs to amount to nothing less than a quantum leap in our understanding of what life is all about, for humanity's previous worldview has been sorely inadequate. Life is not about acquisition. It is not about appeasing one's desires and needs. It is not about lobbying to get one's way. It is not about being victimized or bullying another. It is not about being afraid or causing fear. It is not about seeking pleasure or inflicting pain. It is not about taking control of another or being controlled oneself. It is not about proselytizing personal beliefs. It is not about problems with race or sex or war or governments or culture or territorial borders. Ultimately, it is not even about religion. Simply stated, life is a process of personal growth and development. It is a required transformational process that has been in effect since the dawn of time and will be underway until each soul has passed through every portion of the curriculum.

This change in our collective worldview is not only necessary, it is also inevitable. The reason is because the truth about who we are can no longer be contained within the confines of what we once thought about ourselves. With greater and greater frequency, this single fact has repeatedly led individuals from countless backgrounds, cultures, and faiths to sense and to predict "the end of the world." Although it is true that the world as we know it is coming to a close, it is not that the world is literally ending; rather, it is that our perception of the world and ourselves is in the throes of a complete and radical transformation. When this shift has arrived, we will no longer think ourselves to be what we never really were.

During this time of transition, we stand at a crossroads, both individually and collectively. We can either fight against the inevitable, becoming all the more focused on our limiting and erroneous beliefs, or we can embrace the change and allow our perception of truth to expand along with us. When this change is complete, we will look back on our previous worldview and see it simply as a step in our collective learning process—a stage that we passed through rather than the reality where we ended up.

As it is now, our limited worldview suggests one of two fundamental possibilities about the nature of humankind for much of the world. The first is that life is accidental and random, implying that there is no God and that we are nothing more than physical bodies. The second is that there is a God and He is all-loving, but for reasons we may not understand, He is conditional in that love. He is also all-forgiving, but only within a certain period of time. Nor does He play favorites, unless one refuses to do things His way. Even now, certain logical assumptions suggest that neither of these possibilities is justifiably defensible.

The structure and harmony of the universe, the cyclic nature of all of life, and the universal laws we can perceive in action tend to indicate that the cosmos follows design more so than accident. In our own lives, the fact that we possess the capacity to dream, the ability to hope, and the capability to inspire others to go beyond their perceived limitations suggests that there is much more to us than a physical body.

In terms of the conflicting nature of God, does it not seem problematic that, if the purpose of life is simply to receive the same eternal reward or punishment, for some unknown reason the Creator has visited upon us very different tests? For some, that test may be like an easy math problem that requires only the ability to add and subtract, but for others that test is like a complex algebraic equation that only the most gifted in mathematical theory and computation could even begin to decipher. One person's life may be filled with minor struggles and pain, while another's seems fraught with tragedy, misfortune, and unspeakable horror. This limited worldview would have us believe that a Creator who designed the intricacies of the galaxies could send a child to a Mahatma Gandhi or a Reverend Billy Graham and hope for the same level of success as a child He sent to a Joseph Stalin or a Reverend Jim Jones. Does this really seem Godlike to anyone?

What if the apparent randomness of life weren't random at all, but instead were a purposeful unfolding of experiences, thoughts, desires, and lessons that originated at the level of the soul? What if we were active participants in the creation of every element of our lives rather than simply the recipient of them? What if the Creator were at least as equitable and fair as a loving parent who didn't play favorites with her or his children? What if God were truly all-loving, ever-merciful, and eternally supportive, providing a firm foundation for each of His children to live and grow and become all that they were meant to be?

These premises—that we stand at the brink of a new understanding of the nature of humankind and that there will be an inevitable shift in our worldview—are both explored in much of the work of Edgar Cayce, the father of holistic medicine and one of the foremost twentieth-century spokespersons for the transpersonal nature of humankind.

Over a period of forty-three years, Cayce gave intuitive readings to people from every religious background and all segments of society. During the course of those consultations, he was able to perceive how individuals literally create the structure of their lives through their thoughts, their deeds, and their interactions with others. Cayce called this storehouse of data that he was able to see "the akashic records"; others have referred to the same information as "the Book of Life" or "God's Book of Remembrance." It was this information that enabled Cayce to describe to individuals how their soul had gained, lost, or—often—experienced elements of both during the course of a series of physical sojourns in the earth.

Rather than seeing life as simply a precursor to an inevitable reward or punishment, the Cayce information saw every life experience as a potentially purposeful and necessary stage of development leading to an almost unfathomable realization of one's true connection to God. A reading told one twenty-six-year-old army sergeant: "For you grow to heaven, you don't go to heaven. It is within thine own conscience that ye grow there." (3409-1) With this as his undergirding perspective, Cayce believed that it was through an individual's life experiences and relationships—accruing over a series of lifetimes—that each person was destined to undergo soul development; grow spiritually; overcome shortcomings, weaknesses, and flaws; and eventually reawaken to the true self.

In 1941, a thirty-four-year-old writer asking a series of philosophical questions dealing with the nature of humankind wanted to know the reason behind the Creation of the universe. In the reading, Cayce replied that it was out of " . . . God's desire for companionship and expression . . . " (5749-14) From this same perspective, the Cayce information describes an incredible possible worldview regarding the purpose of life in the earth and the evolving nature of the soul. For ease of expression, we might call this worldview the Cayce cosmology.

In this cosmology, the destiny of each individual is nothing less than soul growth, transformation, and enlightenment. Essentially, the primary function of the earth is as a testing arena that enables the soul to exercise the dynamics of freedom of choice played out against the influences of cause and effect, and to experience whatever understanding and development have already taken place. Although Cayce definitely saw the prospect of soul retrogression (loss) in any given life, generally each lifetime allows for the possibility of advancement in learning. In fact, the readings contend that wherever a person finds him- or herself in the present, that very situation has the potential to be a purposeful one; whether or not the person decides to use the present as a positive learning experience, however, is always a matter of free will.

Because the nature of the soul is spiritual, not physical, it is erroneous to believe that the earth offers the only learning curriculum undertaken by each soul. Instead, Cayce's cosmology describes "sojourns in consciousness" in which the soul chooses to experience focused lessons in what might be called "awareness development." These lessons do not take place in physicality but in other dimensions of consciousness. With this in mind, Cayce informed a group of approximately thirty people who had gathered for a reading in 1933: *"For the earth is only an atom in the universe of worlds!"* (5749-3) Echoing the New Testament (John 14:2), Cayce told another individual, "'In my Father's house are many mansions'— many consciousnesses, many stages of enfoldment, of unfoldment, of blessings . . . " (2879-1)

Cayce advised others that it was also a mistake to believe that our solar system is the only place in the cosmos in which souls are undergoing a developmental process. However, once a soul enters the earth, there is apparently a mandatory lesson that must be attained before the soul is free to continue its curriculum elsewhere. Essentially, that lesson was described as being one of love and service. On other occasions, the readings used biblical terminology to describe that lesson: "For the whole law is to love the Lord with all thy heart and soul and body, and *thy neighbor as thyself*." (1603-1)

In Cayce's worldview, the inevitable destiny of every soul is to become cognizant of its true individuality while maintaining an awareness of its oneness with God. For all of humankind, this state of enlightenment is seemingly achievable in one of two ways: either by learning the lesson of love and then moving on to other stages of consciousness development or by literally attaining perfection in the earth. Of the thousands of individuals who received readings from Edgar Cayce, fewer than twenty were told that they had so mastered the lesson of love that another earthly incarnation would not be necessary unless they chose to return. Apparently, there are "many mansions" in which they could continue their individual growth process. In terms of manifesting perfection in the earth, the example repeatedly cited by the readings was that of Jesus.

In 1944, a fifty-three-year-old housewife named Agnes[2] contacted Edgar Cayce and inquired as to why she had come into life with such a broken physical body. For much of her life, she had suffered from heart, back, hearing, and intestinal problems, often causing her severe pain. In spite of these problems, she had managed to take care of a home and family and raise two sons. She obtained a life reading and was told that her soul had made tremendous strides in spiritual development for

---

[2]For the most part, all names used within this volume have been changed to maintain confidentiality.

she had " . . . advanced from a low degree to that which may not even necessitate a reincarnation in the earth." (5366-1) Not that she was perfect, for she wasn't, but somehow she had learned how to love. Her present difficulties were traced to a low point in her earthly sojourns when she had been a companion of Nero and had taken part in the physical persecution of individuals associated with the early Christian Church. From that experience, Cayce advised her that she was now "meeting self" in terms of her own pain and suffering. Aside from that one period of soul retrogression, however, Agnes was told that throughout her earthly incarnations, she had generally been of service to others in her attempts to be of service to God. As a result, in spite of her physical pain, she had still managed to love, striving to hold to a high ideal and frequently assisting others in doing the same. For that reason, when asked to comment on her abilities, Cayce told her:

Who would tell the rose how to be beautiful; who would give to the morning sun, glory; who would tell the stars how to be beautiful? Keep that faith! which has prompted thee. Many will gain much from thy patience, thy consistence, thy brotherly love.

In spite of how Agnes's life and physical circumstances might have appeared to others, the reading assured her that she had accomplished much.

Within the vast repository of the Cayce material, those factors that lead to a person's soul growth or retrogression in any given lifetime are indexed by case history for ease of reference. In addition to service and love, qualities that prompt soul growth include consistent application, establishing spiritual ideals, developing the will, positive human relationships, personal attunement, selflessness, and cultivating virtuous traits such as patience, forgiveness, understanding, and tolerance. The flaws and weakness pointed out as leading to soul retrogression and failure include self-gratification; self-exaltation; selfishness; intolerance and condemnation; indecision and laziness; creating contention, oppression, and strife in the lives of others; holding grudges or seeking revenge; and being too material minded. Negative traits also include such attitudes and emotions as spite, stubbornness, self-pity, and resentment.

Rather than thinking that the soul is somehow separated or disconnected by each of its earthly experiences, the Cayce readings emphasize the ongoing process of life. Because the soul is eternal, life does not begin and end with each physical incarnation. For ease of understanding, imagine for a moment that the soul is like an individual's entire lifetime and that each period of that person's life is like a different incarnation. There may be a period of childhood, of going to school, of being a parent, of having a job or a series of jobs, etc. Although the core individual does not radically change, outward identity frequently changes. It is not that each life begins anew like a blank slate, but rather that the soul takes with it talents, experiences, relationships, and weaknesses from one lifetime to the next. All weaknesses need to be overcome or transformed, while all strengths need to be further cultivated and expressed. This fact is repeatedly illustrated in the case histories of individuals who received readings.

One woman learned that she had lost spiritual ground centuries ago during a lifetime in India because she had often forced others to accept her personal beliefs and religious tenets. However, that same ability to persuade and mold others had been transformed during a Colonial American incarnation in which she had cultivated the talents of a teacher and instructor and had been instrumental in directing the lives of young people (2910-1).

A very small, thin, frail-looking shoe salesman who suffered from a number of physical problems, including anemia, learned that he had abused his physical prowess, beauty, and strength during a Roman incarnation when he had often subjugated others to his own will. Conversely, during that same incarnation, he had often found favor with the opposite sex by his desire to be of service. For that reason, in the present, women often found occasions to be kind to him. At the same time, however, he frequently attempted to be too controlling with members of his own family, including his wife (1629-1).

In another instance, a thirty-five-year-old psychologist learned that his innate talents for counseling and diplomacy were the result of a number of past-life experiences. In a lifetime after the American Revolution, he had acted as a liaison between the United States and Britain. Although a soldier during the Crusades in another lifetime, he had come to appreciate and admire many individuals of the Moslem faith from whom he had learned brotherly love. His appreciation of various cultures and ideologies was enriched during an earlier period in ancient Egypt, when he had made a study of various teachings and tenets of the then-known world. At the same time, however, this psychologist possessed a tendency toward self-indulgence and self-aggrandizement that had arisen during a Persian incarnation, when he had been in a position of leadership. That same tendency remained with him in the present and needed to be overcome. Years later, his third ex-wife—he would eventually have five—filed a follow-up report that confirmed his propensity for self-indulgence. By her account, during their ten years together, he had repeatedly displayed an incredibly overdeveloped sex drive and a very serious problem with alcohol (1135-1).

Cayce was adamant that the New Testament declara-
tion " . . . for whatsoever a man soweth, that shall he also
reap" (Galatians 6:7) was not simply a quaint saying but
was, instead, a statement of fact and a universal law regarding how the universe really works. For example, an
unhappy thirty-three-year-old actress inquired about
why her life had been filled with a series of broken ro-
mances, rejections, and the experience of having a broken heart. A reading suggested that in her most recent
incarnation she had been a saloon entertainer and had
found occasion to repeatedly toy with men's emotions,
frequently making " . . . for sorrow in the hearts and in
the experience of many." (1300-1) Her present difficulties were simply a learning experience in response to her
having done the same thing to others. As she learned to
keep her heart, mind, and soul in alignment with spiritual ideals, learning a lesson where she had once fallen
short, Cayce promised her "years of happiness and joy
and peace."

In spite of the inevitability of having to meet the consequences of our previous choices, in Cayce's cosmology life is not fixed or destined. Although we constantly
draw individuals and circumstances to us as a result of
choices from the past, we continually cocreate the experience of our life (and our perceptions) through how we
choose to respond in the present. From the readings'
perspective, karma is only soul memory; it is not destiny. The way we choose to respond to that memory and
our present-life experience actually determines the next
probabilities and potentials drawn to the soul's learning
agenda.

During the course of a past-life reading, Cayce told
people only about those incarnations that were having a
direct influence on their present experience. Frequently,
when people received follow-up readings about their

past lives, Cayce discussed additional lives that were then affecting them. When an eighteen-year-old girl named Rachel wrote Edgar Cayce to inquire why all of her incarnations had not been explored in her reading, leaving great gaps of history unaccounted for in her soul's record, he wrote:

> That there are many centuries that elapsed from one appearance to another is not unusual in this information, for one reason, as the information says, there may have been and possibly were other appearances during that time, but the activities at that time or at such an appearance was not of a nature to be of any great influence in your experience just at this time, any more than any one day you attended Dallas Academy has an influence on some problem that you may be working in physics now, but there may come a time in your experience that what you gained at that time or the experience that you had will be necessary as the background—do you get me? Case 259-8 Report File

The case history for this same individual demonstrates why the human will remains the strongest factor in shaping an individual's present life in spite of reincarnation and the number of lifetimes affecting a soul in any given experience. During Rachel's life reading, Cayce told her that because of a series of experiences her soul had undergone in Colonial America, Greece, Persia, and Egypt, she had developed an innate appreciation for freedom and liberty. Because she had been closely associated with a number of founding families in Jamestown, Virginia, she had learned the skills of an excellent politician. As a result of her vocation during the Trojan Wars, she possessed talents in speaking, writing, and artistic expression. However, her potentially greatest path of serving others came from her experience in ancient Egypt, when she had created one of the earliest forms of sunglasses out of colored, polished glass, protecting people from the glare of blinding sands. Her best vocation in the present would be to help people with their sight.

In terms of other advice regarding her life's direction, Cayce counseled her to cultivate many friendships and associates in her life. He warned her specifically against getting married, however—unquestionably because of past-life influences that would inevitably manifest. He told Rachel that, for her, marriage " . . . would bring the character of hardships that would break the purposes in the inner self." Her best course of action would be in helping others, which would, in turn, enable her to discover peace, happiness, and true joy in living.

In spite of what was considered at the time to be an "inappropriate" woman's role, within five years Rachel's strong sense of independence led her to become an optometrist, and she opened her own office. In fact, she became one of the first women in her state to do so and managed to brush aside all the jokes and wisecracks questioning her role choice. In 1942, after opening her practice, she fell in love and wrote Edgar Cayce to explain that she was about to get married and wished " . . . with all my heart you were here to talk over what I am about to do." He responded by reminding her of what her life reading had advised and encouraged her to read it again and approach the decision with prayerful and careful thought. In the end, he assured her to "Know that I am with you and for you, whatever decision you make." Rachel got married within that same month.

By all accounts, Rachel and her husband were extremely happy. Unexpectedly, however, five months after their marriage, he was drafted, and Rachel expressed how, almost as suddenly as it had begun, her dream had stopped. In order to keep herself busy, in addition to her job as an optometrist she went to night school to continue her graduate studies. What spare time she had was spent crocheting. As the months passed and gave way to a year, Rachel became depressed over the separation and the fact that all she knew about her husband's condition was that he was somewhere in England. He was not much of a letter writer. Two years after he was drafted, she wrote Edgar Cayce to state that she had learned more about her husband's work and associates in a letter from a family friend than she could have learned in fifty letters from her husband:

> [He] is one person who really doesn't know how to write. He says three things in every letter (1) I am well, tired, or sleepy. (2) I will be so glad when all of this is over and I can come home. (3) I miss all of you so much. And that is generally all . . .
>
> Sometimes I shudder to think of the two strangers who will meet when he comes home . . . but that is crossing bridges before the road reaches them . . . and it can't be done successfully. So . . . I'll wait. And patience has never been one of my virtues. 259-8 Reports

When Rachel's husband finally returned from the war after thirty-nine months abroad, they apparently had their share of difficulties in coming back together. In part, it proved difficult for her husband to focus on the demands of his job and at the same time reacquaint himself with his wife. In 1946, Rachel encouraged her mother to obtain a copy of Rachel's life reading in order to see how the information in it was being fulfilled. Eventually, after three years of being back together, Rachel and her husband had a son. Four years later, a second son was born to the couple. Unfortunately, shortly after his birth, the child developed spinal meningitis and lived the rest of his life as an invalid.

Rachel's marriage continued until 1969, when her husband suddenly dropped dead. In a subsequent report, Rachel described how she had been startled after her husband's death to see Edgar Cayce (then deceased for almost twenty-five years) standing at the foot of her bed. By her own account, he told her: "This door closes, another will open. Go get your life reading and read it." (259-8 Reports) Years later she would state, "He was right, for spiritually my life turned around from that moment." Ten years later, when both of her sons died unexpectedly the same year, she maintained her sanity by continuing her work routine, attempting to help others, and striving to be an emissary of joy, happiness, and peace, as had been outlined in her reading in the first place. According to the notes on file, she was still practicing as an optometrist well into her seventies. Although a number of tendencies were inevitable in Rachel's life, her actual future was integrally connected to her will and with what she chose to do with her present opportunities.

In order to begin a life reading, the person conducting the readings for Edgar Cayce (usually his wife, Gertrude) would give a suggestion that enabled him to tune in to the soul history of the person and access the relevant information from the akashic records. In part, that suggestion stated that he would be able to provide "the former appearances in the earth's plane, giving time, place, name and that in that life which built or retarded the development for the entity, giving the abilities of the present entity and to that which it may attain, and how." (254-21 and others) Once he had obtained that information, Cayce would respond, "Yes, we have the records here of that entity now known as or called [giving the individual's name]." Thereafter, Cayce would describe soul strengths and weaknesses and provide an explanation of those lifetimes that were having the greatest bearing upon the present.

In addition to the will being an irrefutable factor in the process of soul growth, Cayce emphasized the importance of establishing spiritual ideals with which an individual could direct and evaluate the course of a life.

In 1944, he told a fifty-one-year-old woman that one of the first priorities she needed in her life was to set an ideal. Apparently the woman had a propensity to gossip and to make slighting comments about others. Obviously that tendency was causing a strain in her personal relationships.

During the course of her reading, Cayce mentioned that the woman had exhibited this same frailty in a previous life, when her motto seemed to be "I'll forgive you but I won't forget it," prompting her to speak unkindly of those with whom she was having difficulties. He told her to remember that any fault she observed in others was actually a reflection of the same problem she possessed within herself—otherwise, she would have been unable to perceive it with such clarity in the first place. Instead, she needed to refocus her perception, learning how to minimize the faults she saw in others while magnifying their virtues. As she established an ideal against which she could measure her own actions, her life would inevitably begin to change:

> But if the entity will take self in hand and just don't say, don't do anything about or to another that you would not like to have others do about you, you will find there will be a change in the outlook, there will come to thee opportunities, possibilities that have been denied. For the law of the Lord is perfect and it converts the soul. And when the soul is converted the mind and body changes and leads in the straight and narrow way. 5255-1

At the heart of this spiritual transformation process is the necessity for personal application. Frequently, the readings admonished people to simply begin doing what they knew to do or to apply guidance that had previously been given. While reviewing the past lives of an architect, Cayce informed the individual that he had once been a creator and a lover of all kinds of art and sculpture during a Grecian incarnation. The man had gained in that experience for his efforts at presenting ideals to others. His failure had come, however, by not applying those very ideals in his own life (2108-1).

In another instance, a forty-nine-year-old man inquiring about his health and asking how he might be of greater assistance to humankind was told:

> . . . It is not how much one knows that counts, but how well one applies that it knows; in just being, doing, thinking, that which is pointed out to self through such constant, consistent, *practical* dependence upon the Creative Forces that have promised ever to meet one—every one—when sought. And there will come that which is for the greater development in the soul forces of such an one that seeks. 270-33

The Cayce information on spiritual growth maintains that one of the greatest lessons facing all of humankind is one the readings identified as "cooperation." Amazingly, that lesson is not simply gaining an understanding of how to agree or work with other people; instead, it is a state of being that somehow sets aside personal agendas, beliefs, motives, and desires and enables an individual to become an agent of spirituality in the lives of others. In other words, true cooperation is learning to work with God so that the Creator can work through you. This notion that the Creator desires to become an active participant in each person's life was no more clearly described than in the case of a small group of individuals from Norfolk and Virginia Beach, Virginia, who began receiving a series of readings from Edgar Cayce starting in 1931. Coming together as a "study club" to explore psychic and personal development, the group was promised by Cayce that they could become "light to a waiting world" (262-2) if they simply worked at practically applying spiritual principles in everyday life. The group met for years, receiving readings and discussing such topics as soul development, meditation, prayer, and service. In the end, not only had the group members learned how to cooperate with *spirit* in their everyday lives, but they also ended up compiling a series of essays regarding the lessons they had explored and their personal experiences. That compilation was published in 1942 as *A Search for God* and is still being studied by small groups around the world, making Cayce's prediction that they could become light to the world both personally and globally significant.[3]

Rather than implying that a close connection to spirit is somehow dependent upon religion, dogma, or personal beliefs, the readings are adamant in their stance that the Creator's unconditional love is available to everyone without exception. To be sure, even in Cayce's cosmology, it is understood that the more frequently an individual attunes to spirit, the more successfully that person will be able to experience God's presence, but achieving that level of awareness exists in potential within each individual. In fact, the readings suggest that every single soul will eventually complete the entire curriculum, achieving soul growth and obtaining personal

---

[3]A further discussion of this group and the transformational lessons they received is covered in greater detail in the chapter "Light to a Waiting World."

enlightenment in the process. With this destiny in mind, Cayce asked a thirty-five-year-old attorney, "Can the will of man continue to defy its Maker?" (826-8) When one considers our inevitable destiny as children of a loving God, it is sadly ironic that many religious movements preaching the existence of an all-loving Creator continue to be adamantly opposed to the notion that everyone will eventually make it.

Ultimately, only one thing stands between each individual and a personal awakening: the human will. This thought becomes even more sobering when it is taken into account that in Cayce's cosmology, out of the entire cosmos, humankind stands out for a reason. In exploring how the human creature has set itself apart, the readings suggest that the acorn knows the purpose for which it was created. The oak remembers the reason it has been given expression. The angels on high are in tune with the rationale behind their existence. All the animals and plants of the earth maintain an awareness of what they are to be about—except for one. Only humankind has forgotten the purpose behind its creation. What was that purpose? It was simply to become a companion and a cocreator with God.

Spiritual
Growth
Case
Histories

Know that life is a river or a stream which is constant and each appearance is as a pool that may refresh, in which others may be refreshed . . . make the world a better place because ye have lived in it. Ye can only do that by the hour, by the moment, by the day ye live. For ye are not promised more than one day in the physical consciousness at a time. Use it—don't abuse it! 5392-1

What if God were completely loving and the universe were completely orderly? What if everything that transpired in your life were not intended to be some kind of punishment or reward or even some kind of a random act of chance, whether good or bad? Instead, what if every life event were a purposefully chosen experience at the level of the soul, providing you with a possible means of personal growth and soul development? Now in her late sixties and approaching her fiftieth wedding anniversary, Meg Nelson has come to that very conclusion. As a child, Meg confesses, she was very manipulative and selfish and was used to getting her own way. She says, however, that life's events and her own efforts and personal growth have helped her greatly overcome these tendencies. Her experiences as a wife and a mother have proven to be extremely helpful in enabling her to become a better person. In fact, it was with Meg's daughter, Amy, that Meg got to face her own selfishness and the way she used to manipulate others head-on.

Meg tells how Amy, as a child and teenager, was very strong willed and had difficulty getting along with other members of the family. Amy's problems and personal frustrations caused her to leave home early and then to suddenly get married at the age of eighteen. The marriage was short-lived, and Amy soon separated and divorced. It was not long before she married and divorced twice again. Extremely unhappy and finding herself with two young children of her own, Amy expressed her firm belief that her parents had been the cause of all of her problems. In her anger and unhappiness, she found occasion to tell Meg and her husband that she couldn't possibly love either one of them because of how they had raised her.

In spite of all the difficulties they faced with Amy's anger, Meg was convinced that the experience was a purposeful one and that she and her husband needed to continue to be supportive of their daughter. In the face of a relationship fraught with challenges, Meg set aside her own feelings and tried to reach out to the girl. Even when Amy caused the couple emotional strife, Meg never failed to express her love, keeping in touch with Amy, visiting as often as she could, and helping out financially when it was absolutely necessary. Meg began to believe that the best approach to the situation was simply "love expressed." In time, her perseverance paid off. Amy began to change and started to take responsibility for her life. Amy even put herself through school and, according to Meg, today is a registered nurse, a loving mother of two children, and "a very caring person . . . who expresses her love for both of us."

In retrospect, Meg realizes that it wasn't only Amy who helped her to become a more loving and caring person. Since Meg herself was a wife and mother of four children, having to focus on others became a normal part of everyday life for her. In addition to the regular challenges of raising a family, there seemed to be a number of health obstacles that the family had to overcome. Those challenges included a son who had meningitis at the age of two. Another son suffered an accidental gunshot wound to his Achilles tendon at the age of twelve and took more than a year to heal. Their daughter contracted mononucleosis in high school. Also, Meg and her husband were seriously injured in an automobile accident—an event that took them years to completely overcome.

But perhaps the most trying and challenging experiences of her life happened almost thirty years ago, when her husband became interested in another woman. It seems that, early in their marriage, the couple had difficulties communicating and, by their sixteenth anniversary, they had drifted apart. The breakdown in their relationship prompted Meg's husband to become interested in another woman. When Meg discovered what was happening, she confronted him. The couple spent a great deal of time discussing the situation. Meg told him that he had to make a clear-cut choice between his marriage and the other woman. Her husband professed his love for Meg and was adamant that he did not want the marriage to end. The couple worked through the situation, the marriage survived, and Meg says that their relationship is stronger today than ever before. In summing up that experience, Meg believes she was ultimately able to turn it into something helpful:

> I learned that I, too, was at fault in the relationship and must work at being less selfish and more thoughtful of him and his needs. I try to acknowledge him more for the good he does and the good choices he makes. I also learned that I could forgive him for something that I did not think was possible before that time.

Throughout her life, rather than becoming angry at the challenges life has presented her, Meg has simply tried to see life's events as an unfolding learning process. When a neighbor commented that it appeared as if Meg's family was prone to bad luck, Meg was truly surprised:

> I had never even considered anything that had happened as anything except part of life that we all must experience and learn from. We felt the Lord's presence through all that happened and the strength of loving, helpful friends. We always looked ahead, did what was necessary at the time and never looked back. Our children have developed the same attitudes and do not complain or feel victims of circumstance.

When asked to name a soul strength that wasn't learned through life's events but rather seemed to be a part of who she was from the very beginning, Meg states unequivocally that it has to do with working with children. Almost from the time she was born, she remembers an incredibly strong desire to have baby brothers and sisters. She frequently begged her mother to have another child. By the time she was four, whenever she came in contact with a woman who had a baby, Meg would plead to hold the child and play with it. As she grew up, she looked forward to having a large family of her own and found many occasions as a teenager to baby-sit. Her college path included a degree in child psychology and early childhood education. She taught kindergarten and the primary grades for more than thirty years before retiring and now does substitute teaching. As a grandparent, she loves being with her grandchildren. Her lifelong love of young people has convinced Meg beyond any doubt "that I was supposed to work with children."

From the perspective of the Edgar Cayce readings, all of our relationships with one another are the means by which the soul encounters lessons to be learned in the present as well as failures from the past that need to be overcome. For that reason, our relationships are an ongoing process that the soul picks up exactly where they have been left off. The case history of Franklin Wagner; his wife, Julia; and their daughter, Debbie, provides a unique and interesting portrayal of a family relationship brought back together.

When the family came to Edgar Cayce for help, the couple was troubled by the condition of their twelve-year-old daughter, who was prone to epileptic seizures. As a last resort, friends had referred them for a reading. Apparently, much of their time together had been spent in trying to find help for Debbie; her condition was the cause of much concern for the family. Cayce was able to give them the help that they sought. In addition to providing a series of physical readings that outlined treatment for their daughter's illness, the girl's condition was traced to an early American incarnation when she had once misused her body and her talent for intuition. Cayce told the couple that the three had been brought back together in an attempt to overcome this period of soul regression because each had been responsible for what had transpired. In the language of the readings the result was that "each soul must meet its *own* self." (2345-1) Here's how the information from the readings explained the past-life basis for the present-day situation:

During the period of the American Revolution, Franklin and Julia were married, just as they were in the present. As now, Debbie was their daughter. At the time, the couple believed in and worked for the British cause. Their support of the Crown knew no bounds, and the couple convinced their grown daughter to spy for them. Apparently, the girl was quite attractive, and the best means of procuring the information they desired was Debbie herself. Debbie set out to inflame the passions of those men who could supply her with information that could be used against the colonies. Apparently, the Wagners forced their daughter into a life of prostitution, breaking the girl's morals and ideals in the process. Debbie's acute sense of intuition also had been used for the couple's benefit.

In the present, the three had been brought back together as a means of correcting what they had once done wrong. Much of that correction had been made by Debbie's parents now placing their daughter's needs before their own.

It's important to point out that it wasn't necessarily the *deed* of prostitution that led to Debbie's illness in the present; instead, from a soul perspective, it was the *intent*. Another case in point is that of Alice Young, a fifty-four-year-old widow who was told that she had been a dance hall girl in the Old West—involved in many of the same activities as Debbie—and yet her intent had been vastly different. At the time, her life had been one of severe hardships, and she had to resort to working in saloons for her own survival. Even though she was persecuted by some members of the community for her line of work, she never held a grudge or had pity for herself. Instead, she continued to be patient with those who spoke unkindly of her. In that incarnation, Alice had seen her activities as her best means of being of service to others. In many respects, that lifetime had been a helpful experience in her overall soul's journey. The reading informed her that, even now, she could travel to the places she had once lived and would recall within her inner being some of her life experiences by simply hearing the sounds of the water or the rushing of the wind.

In terms of soul retrogression, however, Alice also had lived a lifetime in the Bordeaux region of France. In that experience, her husband essentially abandoned her in order to take part in a military conflict. According to the readings, that experience had brought her much shame, hardship, and personal doubt. At a soul level, she had lost because of frequently losing faith and hope. The one benefit from that experience was that she had gained an inner prompting to rely upon herself and had learned patience in the process.

Alice was informed that her present-life experience could surpass any of those that had gone before. Apparently, she now excelled in her ability to love, to make friends, and to learn to understand others rather than judging them. Because she was given to good works and being of service to others, Cayce told her that her very presence could emanate a healing influence in the lives of all those with whom she came in contact (823-1).

The continuity of a soul's individuality from one lifetime to another was expressed to a forty-one-year-old researcher who was told that the soul is literally eternal. From this perspective, there is really no such thing as death. What humankind perceives as death is simply a process through which the soul changes in consciousness from the material realm to the spiritual. The man was told that in his most recent experience, he had been among a group of warriors who had attacked the Inca Indians. Although he was not interested in simply destroying and overtaking the people of the land, his counsel had been overruled and he had witnessed the horror and barbaric warfare that resulted. Because life experiences remain at a soul level, Cayce told him that he still possessed a deep-seated fear of what individuals can do when prompted by personal aggrandizement and selfish motives. Although the experience had been deeply troubling, it had also led to a soul longing to become a champion of hope and equality among all peoples. That same drive remained within him.

Previous to his Inca experience, he had been an early explorer who had sailed the seas to help map some of the known lands for the Roman Empire. From that experience, he maintained a deep desire to be associated with and working for the government to which he belonged. In the present, he was encouraged to continue to work with the ideal that had often been a part of his personal reflections regarding soul equality. Apparently, that ideal had often been pondered in biblical terms: "Am I my brother's keeper?" He was assured that each soul truly has a duty to all others. He was counseled to look for channels of service in which he could use his research abilities in a constructive way for others and to bring to their awareness an appreciation of their blessings in everyday life (2147-1).

In a very real sense, the Cayce cosmology sees life as a process in which each person is given the opportunity to overcome failures that have been a part of that soul's history. Those failures are not simply erased, providing the soul with a clean slate. Instead, the soul must face former difficulties and inclinations in a manner that gives the person the opportunity to make a better choice in the present. An example is David Peters, who was thirty-three when he obtained a life reading.

Although David had a responsible job as a restaurant manager, he told Edgar Cayce that he was just getting his life back together because of a troubled past. Evidently, from a very early age, he often felt in conflict and competition with others. From David's perspective, it appeared others frequently had more advantages and more material possessions than he. In time, he desired to possess what he believed was rightfully his. When he was a young man, that desire had led to a criminal record. By his own admission, he was just now trying to stay on the proper road because of "God and [the] people who have faith in me."

Cayce told David that his desire to possess things that belonged to others had long been a part of his soul history. Previously, he had been a soldier of fortune who had turned to plunder as a way of acquiring things that were beautiful and valuable. According to the reading, this activity had caused "discomfort and disturbances that are *still* a part of thy being." Although his soul history included a lifetime in the Holy Land where he had consecrated his life to the service of God, in an even earlier incarnation he had sought to misuse those same spiritual principles for the acquisition of material things and the gratification of his own carnal desires. He was reminded: "And as ye feed those desires mentally, physically, so they grow." This tendency for selfishness had to be overcome.

This then must be the first consideration of the entity: Know that just as ye are a part of a family, ye are part of a city, a part of the law, a part of the country, a part of the universe.

And unless one is as considerate of others as there is the desire for others to be considerate of self, in that whole relationship, there come turmoils and strifes . . .

Then, study to show thyself approved unto God, a workman not ashamed of thy daily life. Though ye may be in need of those things that would bring the pleasures as some ye see about you, *provide* the needs of thy body in love and in justice and in mercy; for the silver and the gold are the Lord's, and those that love Him shall not beg bread.

Know thy ideal, then, and not as to what others are to do for you as the ideal, but what ye would do for others—in the manner ye would have them do it unto you!

Thus ye may know the face of hope, of love, of brotherly kindness, of mercy.

And do it *all* in patience; for God is the God of patience. 1977-1

David was told that if he continued to keep his life on track, the selfishness that had long been a part of his soul history would be eradicated and great opportunities would inevitably come his way.

Another example of negative soul tendencies being carried from one lifetime into the next is the story of a twenty-three-year-old man who was advised that his intense desire for the opposite sex had often led to his downfall. In one of his previous lives, he had been a trumpeter at the walls of the Holy City of Jerusalem and had gained because of his pursuit of service to others. He had lost, however, because of his intense interest in physical pleasures. His pursuit of physical beauty had also been prominent in a Roman experience when he had been a gladiator and extremely proud of his physical prowess and strength.

According to his reading, he had been involved in "places of amusement of every nature" during the Gold Rush, when he had gained a great deal of material wealth and had been very helpful to other miners. He had been extremely lonely, however, and had apparently sought out frequent female companionship. Throughout many of his incarnations, his thoughts toward women were basically self-serving. In the present, Cayce encouraged him to continue his innate interest in being of service to others, for that was also a part of his soul being. In terms of women, he was advised to completely change his approach: "Treat every man's sister as ye would have *thy* sister treated! Treat every woman as ye think of thy mother!" (1881-1)

A Jewish woman with racial prejudice in the present was told that her bias against people who were not like herself had originated in the Old West when she had been a pioneer and had experienced hardships due to conflicts with the Indian natives. She was told that her present life experience would draw to her circumstances and events that would enable her to overcome this prejudice (as well as some of her other shortcomings) and enable her to realize and appreciate what others had to offer in their respective influence (1192-5).

Because patience had been lost in some of his previous experiences, a thirty-nine-year-old Christian Scientist was told that one of the primary purposes of his present lifetime was to simply learn patience. Prone to anger and rash behavior, he had been a champion of freedom in one of his most notable incarnations, in Colonial America. At the time, he had also been savage and merciless in his dealings with many people. Cayce advised the man that some of those same individuals were now a part of his life in the present and he needed to learn to deal with them completely differently. Inclined to be emotional, he was told to remember that all he did or said would eventually have to be met within himself. Rather than being impatient with others, he was encouraged to minimize their faults and learn to magnify their virtues. From that day forward, his best approach in all of his human relationships would be to work with love and patience (2564-3).

Just as a soul's shortcomings and faults remain a part of the individual until they are overcome, soul strengths that have been acquired in the past can also be drawn upon in the present. The case of Sheila Roberts, a forty-eight-year-old secretary, presents a good example. Cayce told Sheila that, throughout her soul history, she had given of herself to such an extent that she had truly been able to bring a sense of God's all-abiding peace into her own life and into the lives of those with whom she came in contact. In spite of the fact that, throughout her experiences in the earth, she had often been a witness to war, animosity, and prejudice among individuals, rather than becoming a part of this conflict, she had so learned tolerance that in the present she literally served as an example to others.

Her past lives included an experience in England during major hostilities with the Huns and the Gauls. According to Cayce, it was a time when neighbor often fought against neighbor, and it was not uncommon for people to take the law into their own hands. In that period, she had frequently attempted to bring a balanced perspective into the lives of her neighbors while assisting them with their own mental and physical burdens. From that experience, she still possessed the ability to give a sense of her own inner harmony to individuals somehow disturbed by emotional or physical distress.

Sheila had also lived a life among the Jews after the people's return to the Promised Land. In addition to her duties as a handmaiden, she had often attempted to help those less fortunate than herself in the surrounding community. Again, she had gained because of her service to others. Unfortunately, at the time she had also been misjudged by a number of people as to the real motives for her work; for that, she had wallowed in self-pity and her soul had lost.

A lifetime in Egypt had given Sheila the opportunity to live at a time when civilization was attempting to bring together the knowledge and teachings of the world. During that period, there was much civil conflict within the society, enabling her to learn that animosity among people only grows unless it is replaced with love and tolerance. That particular lifetime enabled her to achieve a great deal of soul development.

Sheila apparently overcame the inclination toward self-pity in the present, and Cayce commended her abilities by stating, "Who would dare give the entity counsel when it may counsel so well!" (1143-2) She was encouraged to continue helping individuals awaken to an awareness of their own abilities, and she was told that not only could she help them by her physical contact but also by her thoughts, her prayers, and her meditations. Her soul strengths were such that she could often be used as a channel of blessings to others.

Another individual commended for her efforts at soul development was a twenty-year-old woman named Danette. Cayce actually stated that Danette's growth surpassed that of many individuals. Apparently, the woman's attitude was one in which she always placed others ahead of herself. However, it wasn't that Danette was insecure or lacking in personal self-esteem; she was, by all accounts, a natural leader. Cayce informed her that she would be guided to positions of influence, but because of her strengths, she would never attempt to dominate or control someone else.

Danette's past-life experiences included an incarnation in France when she had been one of the court entertainers and idolized by many of the nobility. In addition to bringing joy and happiness to people—for which she had been financially rewarded—her reading stated that she had used much of her wealth and her advantage as a means of being of service to those less fortunate than herself.

During a lifetime in Greece, she had been active in the Temple of Diana and had held a position of influence. In that experience, she often sought to bring spiritual truths to others. Her intent was to help free people from the toils and bondage of everyday life and give them a greater joy in living. Previously, in an Egyptian temple, she had been employed as one involved in music and song. Once again, her work and dedication to spiritual truths brought happiness and entertainment to many.

Cayce complimented her drive, even in the present, to bring hope, joy, peace, happiness, good cheer, and love into the lives of those with whom she came in contact. Danette was informed that her talents were varied and that she would make a wonderful nurse, a skilled teacher of dramatic arts, or an inspiring storyteller (4500-1).

Another example exploring both soul strengths and weaknesses is the case of a sixty-one-year-old widow named Barbara who received a life reading in 1937 and was told that *many* of her past lives were having a direct influence upon her present experience. Though drawn to sculpture throughout her life, Barbara had never really attempted to explore her own creative talents, apparently because she was somewhat reclusive and withdrew from fully expressing herself. Cayce informed her that part of the reason was because she possessed an innate fear of being misunderstood.

Her past lives included a sojourn as one of the first settlers in upper New York, where she had experienced many physical hardships. From that period, she had gained in personal strength and perseverance. At the same time, however, Barbara had encountered much loneliness, giving her a strong desire for friends and acquaintances, a desire that remained with her even in the present. Much of her ability to love still remained dormant, however.

During a lifetime in the Middle Ages in Germany, Barbara had been left behind as her family and male relations went off to fight for a religious cause. From that lifetime, she had gained the ability to be practical but she had lost because of frequent self-pity—it was an attitude on which she continued to work. In Greece, she had been an artist of note, specializing in sculpture. It was that experience that kept her love of art alive. In addition to her artistic talent, from that same incarnation she had acquired an interest in the pursuit of spiritual truths.

Barbara was told that a lifetime in Indochina had provided her with a variety of experiences in which she had made great strides in soul development, but she had lost as well. The Indochina experience had given her a true awareness of brotherly love, but at the same time she had become very much involved in the pursuit of pleasures and the satisfying of personal indulgences. Previous to that lifetime, she had been adept at esoteric sciences and divination and had used these tools as a means of showing people their true relationship to God.

In summing up her lifetimes, Cayce told Barbara that she possessed much motivation for assisting others with their personal welfare. She had a great deal of artistic talent that was waiting to be tapped. She had an immense capacity to love that needed to find outlets as well. Her deep interest in spiritual truths still resided within her. Barbara simply needed to open up and become more willing to express herself in many directions. She was encouraged to continue her pursuit of spirituality. All these things would provide her with a means to overcome some of the innate influences that needed to be purged from her inner being (1474-1).

From the Cayce files, it is apparent that one of the most important influences affecting whether a soul experiences retrogression or development in any given experience is the intent or motivation behind an individual's actions. In the case of Angela, a thirty-six-year-old artist, Cayce noted how her change in motivations had altered her life experience, even within the same incarnation.

Part of Angela's soul history included being a teacher during the early settling of Long Island. In that experience, she had gained for a period because of her practical service to others in assisting them in daily life. Eventually, her efforts led to some prominence and notoriety. Unfortunately, that notoriety caused her to become somewhat self-centered and interested in bettering her own environment and, as a result, she had lost. Because of the change in her motivation, she eventually alienated herself from the very people she had once tried to help. Cayce told her that, once she had alienated herself from people, she became somewhat isolated and was forced to spend much time in personal reflection, thinking about what had transpired. After a time, the isolation enabled her to regain her perspective and the proper mental attitude, and once again she grew in soul development.

Angela's artistic talent was traced to an incarnation that had coincided with the period when the early Christians were being persecuted for their beliefs. At the time, she had apparently been both the companion and student to one of the most popular artists of the day. The Christian persecutions had troubled her, and she had spent many hours in personal introspection and contemplation trying to understand what prompted individuals to die for their beliefs. That prompting eventually led Angela to investigate spiritual truths for herself.

The beginnings of her spiritual longing were traced to an earlier incarnation in Greece, when she had forsaken the beliefs of her upbringing and had instead pursued religious principles that would eventually form the basis for the Zoroastrian religion. That incarnation had enabled her to learn that worldly goods are only important if they lead an individual to the attainment of spiritual truths. Although that lifetime had brought her material hardships because of giving up her heritage, it had provided her with a spiritual understanding and development that remained with her even in the present.

Angela was advised that she possessed the ability to relate life's experiences through her art. Somehow, people could have an inner awakening about their own life experiences simply by beholding her work. In terms of where she was supposed to turn her artistic expression, she was encouraged to create works that would "bring happiness to others, with a joy of life and its experience ... something of joy, something of hope ... " (431-1) By so doing, she would bring greater joy, peace, and harmony into her own life.

A motivation for the pursuit of material wealth was apparently a driving force in a number of the incarnations given to a forty-eight-year-old dress designer. He was told that this same motivation remained with him. This was one of the factors that had caused him to experience soul loss in his earthly sojourns, in addition to some of the gains he had made.

His abilities with clothing were first traced to a French incarnation when he had attired many members of the aristocracy. He had gained because of his desire to be of service in attiring people. He had lost, however, because of his acquired capacity to clothe people in attire that was known solely for its ability to inflame human passions. His abilities in this regard had gained him a reputation and some measure of financial success. In a lifetime previous to that experience, he had used women simply as lures to undermine the principles of spiritual pursuits of a rival city from which he hoped to obtain material benefit. In an earlier lifetime in Egypt, he had also been involved in creating bodily attire and adornments, assisting people in displaying their position and occupation in life through the clothing that they wore. The man was told that, even now, he possessed a soul tendency that could cause him to pursue material things in preference to his own spiritual nature. The advice was to change this motivation. There was nothing wrong with using his creative abilities, but they needed to be directed into avenues that would provide hope and inspiration, accentuating the beautiful rather than that which was carnal in nature. Apparently, he listened to the advice. According to the reports on file, he eventually turned some of his creative abilities to painting and became involved in all kinds of community projects. In time, he also won several Oscars for his work in the movies (2416-1).

A doctor, who would become prominent for her work in psychiatry and the use of art therapy for addressing emotional problems in children and adults, obtained a life reading in 1933. Her most recent incarnation had been during the Salem witch trials when—as an observer—she had tried to understand the physical causes for those who appeared to be having convulsions and were labeled as possessed. During another experience in Germany, innumerable duties and many obligations in caring for a household had often burdened her. In the fulfillment of her labors, she had often pondered the difference between practical things that might make an individual's life better and spiritual ideals that could provide hope but were not necessarily things of a practical nature. From that experience, she had learned it is not what an individual knows that is of utmost importance; rather, it is how an individual applies what she or he knows that makes for growth in every area of life. In Egypt, she had striven to better the lives of individuals less fortunate than herself, and in Atlantis, she had gained by disseminating spiritual truths to others. When the doctor asked if her reading covered all of her incarnations, Cayce responded: "By no means. These are the ones that influence the most in the present." (444-1)

In 1929, during the course of his life reading, a tailor learned that his lifetime in England carried one of the greatest influences in the present. During that experience, he, too, had been a clothier for the nobility. His talent with clothes and attire originated from that incarnation. Unfortunately, because of his acquaintances, he apparently became somewhat snobbish and began to believe that those in power were more deserving and worthy than the common people. The reading told the man that his desire as a teenager to rule others by power, might, and influence had arisen from that English incarnation. Thankfully, because of his life experiences, he had come to learn that love, honor, reason, and justice were stronger than physical power and might (417-1).

An interesting case presented itself in 1931 when Cayce informed a twenty-two-year-old woman that her lifetime as a Grecian dancer had been wasted and had "counted as naught." At the time, she had used her abilities as a dancer to give much artistic expression to the people. Ordinarily she would have gained for that; however, she had turned her beauty toward satisfying her own desires. The gain and the loss had offset one another, causing the lifetime to have no effect on her overall soul development (543-11). Conversely, a thirty-seven-year-old woman was told that, in a previous life, she had used her talent with dance to bring both pleasure and moral lessons to the people. As an entertainer, she had used dance to demonstrate moral and spiritual truths to her audience (2741-1).

From the readings given to those who sought Cayce's help and assistance, it's evident that soul growth is not necessarily achieved by any great work or by somehow becoming famous or notorious. By far the majority of people who received readings were regular people with everyday lives. In tracing the soul histories for these same people, Cayce gave very few of them past incarnations of any prominence. In the past, they had also been common people with common problems, challenges, hopes, and dreams. From this wealth of information, it becomes apparent that soul growth occurs as a part of the normal life process as people simply try to do the best that they can with the experiences that life draws to them. The readings often told people that the purpose of life wasn't simply to be good; rather, it was to be good for something.

Using the parable of the talents (Matthew 25:14-30), Cayce reminded a sixteen-year-old boy that he needed to be active with his life, using his abilities *for* something rather than simply hiding them from the world. In fact, Cayce told the young man that it was far better to make mistakes in the pursuit of trying to do something positive with his life than it was simply to sit idle: "Better to do even the *wrong* thing than to do nothing." (674-3) Another individual was told, "Then, as to whether there is the development or retarding [regressing] of the soul entity, is dependent upon the manner in which the abilities of the entity are exercised or used." (3420-1) Apparently, just as in the parable of the talents, as one uses abilities possessed at a soul level, even more soul strengths can be expressed; whenever one withdraws from doing the best that one knows, regression is the result. Hundreds of examples of how soul abilities originated in the past and can be traced into the present can be found in the Cayce archives.

For example, an eighteen-year-old man was informed that his even temperament and personality were traceable to a lifetime in Persia when he had been in a position of leadership. In that situation, he had been required to listen to and address the demands and needs of many people. For that reason, he now possessed the talents of a conversationalist, a salesman, a mediator, and an arbitrator—all of which he could draw upon in the present (1912-1).

A woman learned that her ability to make friends came as a result of an Egyptian incarnation. At the time, the country had been in the midst of rebellion and civil war. After the conflict, however, the woman had gone out of her way to befriend those who had been on the opposing side. That ability to reconcile differences and to cultivate friendships still remained a part of her (69-1).

A forty-nine-year-old motion picture executive was told that his aptitude with the media was traced to an Egyptian incarnation, in which he had been minister of communications and had trained emissaries and missionaries to other lands. In addition to his executive abilities, the lifetime had provided him with the opportunity for much soul growth. He was encouraged to use his power to be helpful to others, to pursue his spiritual interests, and to overcome personal insecurities (5463-1).

A man who was employed as a successful furniture salesman discovered that his abilities in sales had resulted from an incarnation defending the Trojan wall, when he had excelled in his ability to meet and speak with people from every walk of life (1739-8).

A fifty-seven-year-old writer and radio broadcaster learned that her talents with communication had been used in a number of previous lives, especially during an incarnation as an Essene. In that period, despite physical hardships, a heavy workload in the Essene community, and frequently being questioned and scoffed at by the Romans, she had labored to preserve spiritual records as a writer and a scribe. Because of her perseverance, she had gained in soul development and grown in grace, knowledge, and an understanding of her relationship to the Creator. She was encouraged to use that same determination in the present in her work in radio and communication to bring an awareness of God's love for His children (1472-1).

Cayce frequently advised individuals to draw upon some of their soul abilities from the past and enable themselves to overcome shortcomings or problems in the present—many of which seemed to contain a past-life basis as well. A thirty-four-year-old chicken farmer was told that her fears and doubts about relationships in the present had originated in her most recent incarnation, when she had been abandoned. Because she had once been a musician in Rome, she was encouraged to put those things that made her fearful into verse and song and to turn those fears instead into inspiring words that could assist others as well as herself (2123-2).

A housewife, who once commented that every member of her family had been helped by the Cayce readings and that she "wouldn't take a million dollars" for her own life reading, was told that her most recent incarnation had been during the Civil War. From that experience, she had gained a determination that caused her to be headstrong at times. In the present, she was encouraged to take her strength of will and direct it into more constructive channels. In a previous incarnation in Spain, she had been a male and a military leader and had gained physically, mentally, and spiritually because of her dedication to a purposeful cause. As a leader, she had been extremely helpful to those in her charge, but she had lacked an awareness of how her efforts could have any effect except a material one. The result was that, in the present, she continued to provide a benevolent influence to those around her, but she was never really satisfied with her life because she lacked an awareness of higher spiritual truths. She was encouraged to pursue spiritual interests, to meditate, and to begin praying daily:

> Here am I, Lord! Purge Thou me from all unright-
> eousness. Make me a greater channel of blessings
> to everyone day by day; not my will but Thine, O
> Lord, be done in and through me. 263-4

A person's ability to continue to learn and grow remains throughout a life. Each segment of a lifetime can provide experiences in which soul strengths can be used and soul weaknesses can be overcome. Life is an ongoing process of soul growth and development. The contemporary story of Anna Stuart provides an example.

In 1944, Anna contacted Edgar Cayce about receiving a reading for her husband. Unfortunately, Cayce died before the appointment could take place. To her surprise, Anna received a letter in the mail explaining Cayce's death and returning the money she had submitted for the reading, even though she had not asked that the money be refunded. She soon joined A.R.E. in 1945 and later reported: "I decided that I wanted to be part of a group that demonstrated such honesty."

For much of her life, Anna has worked as a nurse and a teacher. She believes that her skills at nursing carried over from a previous lifetime, because there were several instances as a young child when she just knew what to do to help someone. One of her earliest memories occurred when she was five and her baby brother was ill with a cold. While her mother was out hanging laundry, her brother woke up coughing. Even now, Anna recalls how sick he appeared and how he just seemed so miserable as he lay crying.

Without giving it a second thought, Anna managed to climb up the shelves of the pantry cupboard and reach a bottle of paregoric, an opium-based medicine, that her mother had placed far out of reach. She gave her brother a dose of the paregoric and then replaced the bottle where she had found it. A short time later, the baby fell back to sleep. However, when her mother came back inside the house, she smelled paregoric on the infant's breath. Realizing what must have happened, she hurriedly called the doctor, fearful that her daughter had poisoned the baby. After the doctor arrived, it became clear that there had been no cause for alarm. Somehow, Anna had known just how much paregoric to give to her little brother, although she admits she "never did it again."

The desire to work with health and medicine stayed with her throughout her childhood. She really wanted to become a doctor, but at the time such a role was almost unheard of for a woman, and she opted for nursing instead. In retrospect, she feels that one of the biggest mistakes of her life was allowing her fears to overrule her deep desire to become a doctor.

In spite of her desire to help people, during the course of her career Anna found that she often was indifferent to individuals' feelings. Early on, through much of her work as a nurse, she also found that, for some reason, she had the opportunity to work with a number of challenging co-workers. On a number of occasions, she found herself stewing and contemplating what she could do as revenge for what someone at work had done to her.

After she began exploring and applying some of the soul development material in the Cayce readings, she noticed how her life began to change. She no longer possessed the desire to "get even" with those with whom she was having difficulties. She stopped being indifferent to the feelings of other people, finding the desire within herself to change and to see all people in a new light. Even some of her most difficult relationships at work changed. Anna recalls with a smile, "After I started applying some of the spiritual information in the Cayce readings, the operating room nurses suddenly became very helpful and unusually nice."

Trained as a nurse and in anesthesiology, she worked twelve years before returning to college for a master's degree in elementary education. Afterward, she taught for seventeen years, obtained a second master's degree, and became a specialist in the teaching of reading.

She was married in 1943 and adopted a six-day-old son in 1946, but her marriage ended in divorce in 1964. A few years later, however, her ex-husband needed her when he became ill, so Anna devoted her time and her nursing skills to help take care of him until he died. She married a second time in 1968 to a man named Wayne. She believes that some of her most meaningful life experiences took place with him. They traveled together, studied together, learned a great deal about spiritual philosophies, and even hosted a spiritual growth discussion group for many years in their home. Anna believes that she learned a great deal by marrying a second time. Wayne was a great teacher and a good example of someone who "magnifies the virtues and minimizes the faults." In fact, she feels that she became a better person for having the opportunity to be with him.

After twenty years of marriage, Wayne also became ill, and she had to nurse a second husband until his death. Even now, Anna recalls what a positive example he provided in spite of his illness:

> He never complained, even while he spent many months dying—still kept up with his reading (talking books) and making jokes. I think I learned that no matter how bad things are (or seem to be), they could be worse. I learned to be thankful and grateful for friends and kindnesses that came my way.

And to extend friendship and kindness to others.

After becoming a widow, Anna became actively involved with the literacy volunteers. Her work of helping others continues to this day. Now in her mid-eighties, she is teaching English to two young women from Taiwan. Even now, she believes there is still more for her to learn. Although she has made some strides with patience and the importance of learning forgiveness, she confesses that she is still trying to learn a very important lesson—the necessity of giving up her need to control life's situations.

In the Cayce cosmology, sometimes a dramatic life change can be the very means by which a soul learns something truly valuable. A contemporary example is the case of Marilyn Bowles who, at seventy-three, says that she has undergone a number of such experiences and believes she is currently in the midst of another. After having raised three children, working through a lifetime of severe problems with her own mother, and settling down with her husband to retire, Marilyn discovered that she is going blind.

Always a visual person, she loves reading, painting, and crafting. Her extreme independence also has made her loss of eyesight a real challenge. Although it is difficult, Marilyn says, "It has really been a blessing in many ways. I have had to give up my independence and rely on others for assistance." Perhaps her source of greatest support has been her husband. He has taken on many of the tasks that Marilyn once did for herself, including cooking, cleaning, and some additional financial responsibilities for the household. When discussing what she has learned from him, Marilyn says: "A better example of unconditional love, I can't imagine. Patience and understanding, he had practiced for fifty years. What a superb teacher and example!"

Besides her blindness, Marilyn admits that her greatest life challenge has been her mother. Throughout her life, there has been friction between the two of them. "Nothing I ever did pleased her." In addition to being negative and critical, the woman never approved of Marilyn's husband. The opportunity to work through the relationship came in 1979, when her mother broke her hip and was forced to move in with the couple. The difficulties between them came to the forefront.

True to his nature, her husband managed to live as best he could with his mother-in-law; however, Marilyn had a very difficult time with the situation. Although she had always been extremely intelligent, Marilyn's mother began doing things that seemed crazy. The older woman began to hide her belongings and then seemed incapable of finding them, or she would simply destroy something and then not be able to use it. Soon after, the couple discovered that Marilyn's mother had Alzheimer's. The situation deteriorated until the older woman's safety was in question and the couple was forced to lock her in her room, letting her out only when she could be with someone at all times. Eventually, Marilyn was forced to admit, "I really hated her and had difficulty even touching her."

In order to cope, Marilyn began working with others who cared for family members with Alzheimer's. She read about the disease and began to study the brain and its functions. When her mother's situation called for twenty-four-hour-a-day care, the couple was forced to put the woman in a nursing home. Marilyn continued her involvement, began actively studying the Edgar Cayce information on soul growth and, in time, began to see her mother in a new light. She knew success had been achieved when "At last I could put my arms around her and really say, 'I love you,' and mean it." Throughout it all, Marilyn believes she has learned unconditional love, patience, understanding, and faith. As for how to confront life's situations, Marilyn says simply, "Look for joy in each day."

This same sense of learning to gain an appreciation for life is expressed in the case of Kristen, a forty-two-year-old woman from West Virginia. Routine life experiences have brought her to a point where she finally appreciates herself and what life has to offer. With some challenge, she has managed to learn patience, in no small measure thanks to her son. She has also learned how to remain calm in situations over which she has no control, and she has found how important it is to remain positive and attempt to cultivate an appreciation for all the beauty that can be seen in nature. Although her life has taken her through common difficulties and frustrations, including divorce and challenges in interpersonal relationships, she now considers herself happy and believes that one of her greatest lessons was to simply realize that "It didn't matter what anyone else thought of me; what mattered was what *I* thought of me." After many years, that realization enabled her to finally tell her elderly parents how much she appreciated them, an experience, Kristen recalls as a very special moment in her life.

One of the most important factors in soul development is a person's capacity to understand the needs of others. This premise is repeatedly demonstrated in the Cayce archives. The readings told one person that "service to others is the highest service to God." (257-10) With this in mind, a twenty-seven-year-old attorney was told that love, tempered with reason, was the motivating factor in all that he did. His nature was traced to a number of previous lives spent in England, Persia, and Egypt. In England, he had been a monk, and although he had spent too much time cloistering himself in personal study, he had properly sought to be of service to those less fortunate than himself. From that period, he also maintained a desire and a reverence for personal study. In Persia, he had gained because of a leadership position that enabled him to be of service to others and to be a champion of law and order. That experience provided him with his present interest in law. In Egypt, he served as a mediator and grew in his capacity to love, his ability to be candid, and his desire to seek cooperation among all people. He had also been a champion of helping people to learn to help themselves. According to his reading, he could draw upon all of these talents (2709-1).

Veronica was a twenty-four-year-old music teacher who was told that, because of her emotional nature, much of her life experience would be based upon her own perceptions. Her life could become very positive or very negative. If she chose to bring happiness and joy into the lives of others through her activities, she would experience a wonderful life. Conversely, if she focused only upon herself, her material needs, and her personal desires, "what a mess may be made out of this experience!" (518-1) In the present, Veronica was encouraged to do those things that would instill spiritual hope into the lives of those with whom she came in contact. She was to do the same thing for herself. In terms of her own emotional nature, she was encouraged to "be joyous in all that thou doest. Smile often, for *smiling* is catching— but sadness drives away."

A twenty-seven-year-old man was told that the reason people so often turned to him for advice and counsel was because he had acquired the talent to be helpful in this regard in earlier incarnations. As a Dutchman, he had once wielded a tremendous and beneficial influence over many people. As a Tibetan Lama, he had assisted others in a practical understanding of the Indian scriptures, the Vedas. Because of his past incarnations, the reading advised the man that he still wielded an extremely helpful influence over people and that no soul would ever be the same after having spoken with him (315-4).

In discussing the nature of the akashic records from which Cayce obtained his information, the readings make it clear that this data is not obtainable only by a psychic. From Cayce's perspective, this material is actually available at all times to every individual. The "shadows" of these records can literally be seen in how people speak, how they think, and how they interact with others. These very same records are somehow accessible by the subconscious mind, through dreams, reveries, and intuitive experiences.

An interesting example occurred in 1931, in the case of a sixty-four-year-old Hindu yogi and scientist who requested a reading. Even before receiving his reading, the man had an experience that provided him with a number of the same incarnations explored by Cayce. According to the man's report, he had a dream that seemed to access the akashic records of his own soul history:

> I was sitting at a desk and a globe of the world was standing before me on the desk. I wanted to find out some place where I had lost something very dear to me. So I went on passing my finger on the surface of the globe map to locate the place. I started somewhere on the east coast of this country—somewhere near Philadelphia, then passed my finger on the province named Tuscany? in France, thence to Alexandria, then through Egypt, Arabia, and then to the west coast of India somewhere towards the south. Though realization then come to me that I could not go further, so I passed the finger on the west coast of India from that southern point and went towards the north of India—beyond

Karachi. While my finger passed over Bombay, it seemed I momentarily forgot that Bombay was the place where I was born in my present existence. At the last halting point—Karachi—I felt greatly disappointed in failing to meet my objective and for a moment puzzled to know what to do next. At that moment, I heard a distinct voice as if commanding me to go back. I then passed my finger from Karachi to westward—over Persia, Palestine, Germany, and arrived back at the same province "Tuscany" in France. Thence my finger passed on to the southwestern states of America, New Mexico, Arizona, Utah, Nevada, and upper California. From there the finger all of a sudden traveled back eastward and stopped at some place north of Boston and then I suddenly woke up. 358-3 Reports

When he received his reading, he learned that his most recent incarnation had, in fact, been during the early settling of Philadelphia, when the colonists were making treaties with the Indians. At the time, he had been of service to many and had gained, but eventually he had created contention among various groups for his own benefit and material gain; for that, he had lost. Cayce told the man that he possessed an innate love for the United States and for the principles of freedom that it represented. However, rather than being born in the states in the present, he had chosen to be born in India in order to rekindle the spiritual purposes that had earlier been a part of his soul's journey. As an adult, however, he had been drawn back to the states.

During a lifetime in Arabia, he had lost and gained for the same reasons as in Philadelphia. He had sought to be of service, attempting to aid individuals in creating a better life for themselves, but at the same time he had lost for turning the wish for a better life into the satisfying of personal desires. Later in that incarnation, the reading stated, he had come in contact with spiritual truths that had provided him with opportunities for much soul growth, especially as he attempted to relate those same truths to others. It was this period of his Arabic incarnation that could be the most helpful in his present life.

Previously, he had served as a high priest in one of the temples in Egypt. In that capacity he had done much to bring spiritual truths to others. Some of those truths, however, he had purposely deviated in the direction of the occult. In the present, he was encouraged to learn the difference among the spiritual, which can lead to inner awakening; the mystic, which can be extremely helpful unless it becomes simply a method of attaining personal experiences; and the occult, which often partakes of influences other than those that are spiritual. He was also advised to continue his pursuit of the spiritual side of humankind's development rather than the material side.

After receiving his life reading, the man told Cayce, "You will no doubt see that information given by you and what I saw in my vision tally on most points—particularly regarding my previous existence."

From Cayce's perspective, every lifetime provides each individual with experiences through which the soul can become more aware of its true relationship to the Creator. Ideally, those experiences enable the soul to overcome some of the faults and tendencies that have been a part of that individual's history. But growth is not necessarily something that can be seen nor is life circumstance necessarily related to an individual's possible development or regression. In a number of instances, Cayce told people, "God looketh upon the heart." (2905-3 and others) What an individual possesses inside is of far more consequence than appearance to others.

As a case in point, on several occasions, a fifty-eight-year-old architect asked his wife, "What good is it to be honest and straight, when almost all around you, you see others thriving on what should not be?" In spite of his dedication to higher principles, he had become discouraged by the fact that he often saw individuals who seemed to be motivated by selfishness and power succeeding financially, whereas he had not. During the course of his life reading, the man was told that he had made such strides in spiritual growth that he might not have to return to this earth plane unless he chose to do so. He was commended for always living a life of high ideals in spite of a variety of opportunities in life in which he could have been selfish. His reading encouraged him not to be discouraged by life's events because he had succeeded in learning far more than most people. For that reason, he was advised to keep sticking to his principles. His wife later reported that Cayce's encouragement for continuing how he had been living all along had made him very, very happy (322-2).

What if life were truly a process of soul growth and development? What if we were not here simply to be good or bad and then receive our accompanying reward or punishment? What if it were our heritage as children of an all-loving God to be good for something, becoming channels of our Creator's compassion, love, service, and hope to those individuals who are sent our way? What if everything that happened to us in life could become a purposeful experience, if we simply chose to make it so?

Spiritual Growth Through Meeting Self

3

For constantly is the soul-entity meeting self in its activities, in its relationships. And what it does about creative influences in its experience makes for that which either becomes a developing or a retarding.   1604-1

What if everything you ever did somehow came back to you? What if this boomerang action were designed to enable you to face how every element of your life had affected someone else? What if you were truly held accountable for all of your actions, for all of your words, even for all of your thoughts? What if this accountability were not some kind of a universal judge and jury, but rather, a portion of your own soul that kept track of everything within your being that was out of alignment with spiritual wholeness, so that it could become transformed? What if this transformational process were inevitable for every soul? What if this process of meeting yourself truly had your best interests at heart?

In the Cayce cosmology, too often we are short-sighted in attempting to discover the basis for our life's challenges and problems. A thirty-seven-year-old book-keeper who was in the midst of marital difficulties was advised: "For each soul, each entity, *constantly* meets self. And if each soul would but understand, those hardships which are accredited much to others are caused most by self. *Know* that in those you are meeting *thyself!*" (845-4) On another occasion, a thirty-one-year-old woman who had a serious problem with facial neuralgia inquired, "Please give the origin of all of this trouble." The reading replied, "It began about thirty-five thousand years ago! This is the trouble!" (3517-2) It then proceeded to encourage her to follow through on the therapeutic suggestions that had been outlined for her treatment.

The sense that every life experience can be seen as a learning process if only an individual will choose to do so is clearly illustrated in the case of Lorraine, a forty-eight-year-old woman who requested a life reading. Twelve years earlier, she had been stricken with polio encephalitis and was unable to walk from that time on. The debilitating nature of her condition had taken its toll on her and her family, and a number of different treatments had been sought. Finally, Lorraine came to Edgar Cayce for help. She was convinced that there was something standing in the way of her own treatment because doctors had been unable to assist her. In her letter, she wrote, "I feel increasingly that there must be some mental and spiritual block that must be removed before much physical progress can be made . . . "

During the course of her reading, Cayce counseled the woman to begin seeing her condition as a purposeful experience, one that would enable her to overcome a soul frailty that had occurred when she had lived in the

Roman Empire. He reminded her gently, "For as one soweth, so one reaps; else the very Divine would be mocked among the children of men." (1504-1) The reading informed Lorraine that she had been a member of the emperor's court and had very much enjoyed the games of "sport" in which the Christians had been thrown to the lions. She was told, "And the entity *laughed* at those who were crippled by such activities; and lo, they return again to thee!" She was now having the opportunity to meet within herself some of the same pain and suffering that she had once made light of in others.

To make the situation even more interesting, the reading advised her that some of the family members who were now taking care of her had once been the same individuals she had watched suffer and die in the arena. It suggested that she attempt to see the situation in a completely new light: "How blest then art thou, that there are those close to thee that ye once laughed at; that are patient, that are kind, that are gentle with thee!" The biggest obstacle to Lorraine's healing was herself. The challenge seemed to be one in which she was supposed to learn to become loving, patient, and kind with those who attempted to help her—in spite of her challenges and pain. She had taken her family for granted, and Cayce suggested that she could "give much, much the more to those about thee . . . "

As physical treatments, the readings recommended frequent electrical stimulation to the muscles and a variety of therapeutic massages. Cayce suggested that if she followed the treatment, began meditating, changed her attitude, and attempted to cultivate the same degree of loving service that was being shown to her by others, the very cells of her body could become rejuvenated.

After receiving the reading, Lorraine wrote, "This is to thank you from the bottom of our hearts for the reading. You don't know what it is doing for us. This happens to be a very troubled moment, and that crystal-pure well of thought is holding us together." Three weeks later, Lorraine wrote again and stated that she had already felt the effects of treatment and was hoping for a quick recovery. She was convinced that her physical trouble was only temporary and would be healed very rapidly. Cayce wrote back and asked her to ponder the following:

> ... the existent conditions are the effect of long-submerged hindrances that at last found expression in a way that requires you to depend upon others, the thing mentally that you hated, and as the Psalmist said, "That which I hated has come upon me." As it has been a growth, and the mind is the builder, so to come out of it also must be a growth. Would a momentary healing bring the lesson that is to be learned?

Cayce encouraged Lorraine to keep him posted on her progress and to find ways in which she could be "good for something," especially in the lives of those who were tending to her needs.

Three months later, Lorraine wrote to say that she was still very happy with the mental and spiritual advice that had been provided in her reading, but that she was somewhat disappointed in the physical information because, "I feel increasingly convinced that if there is to be any recovery, the cure will be instantaneous and bordering on the miraculous." Although a number of letters were exchanged between Lorraine and Edgar Cayce in 1938, by year's end he received no further communication from her.

It appears that Lorraine was unable or unwilling to follow the advice that Cayce had given her. In 1974, Lorraine's daughter got in touch with Cayce's Association a year after her mother's death and requested a copy of her mother's reading. It was sent, along with a letter of inquiry asking for an update on what had happened to Lorraine since the course of her reading. The daughter's letter stated, in part:

> You ask[ed] me to make any comments relevant to the Cayce reading on my mother. She suffered from poliomyelitis and many painful and frustrating conditions during her life. Edgar Cayce, according to the reading, was of the opinion that she could have been healed. To the best of my knowledge, she did not follow through with his advice and told me later that he had given her nothing more helpful than that she was paying off a karmic debt. She lived, in spite of cancer, arthritis, diverticulitis, chronic bladder inflammation, etc., etc., to the age of eighty-three, dying quite senile. It is most regrettable to her family that she did not make the total effort at self-healing which was available to her . . .

On another occasion, a thirty-nine-year-old, unmarried hairdresser obtained a life reading and was told that her challenges with relationships were apparently due to a series of past lives that was still affecting the present. Cayce told her that she often seemed to seek out "disturbing" relationships in the present because she was lonely, very unwise in love, and apparently meeting a situation from an earlier incarnation.

Previously, she had been a Grecian maiden who was an entertainer and possessed great beauty. In an attempt to better her position, she had often ensnared the hearts of men who might help her gain position, place, or power. She was now meeting that experience in the present. Cayce suggested that she needed to change her approach to people as well as her perception of herself. She was encouraged to discover the talents and abilities within herself rather than looking at people in terms of what they might be able to do for her. She also was encouraged to begin interacting with others differently. Cayce said that his advice in this regard was applicable to everyone: "Would that each soul would make that as a rule, a determining factor, 'In each contact, each conversation with another, I will leave a thought, an idea, that will better that individual.'" (2438-1) The reading told her that if she followed this advice, she would inevitably find the love in relationships that she was seeking.

A contemporary example of relationship difficulties is seen in the story of Ken Archer. Ken is a forty-eight-year-old supervisor at a water treatment facility. After having been through three very emotional relationship breakups, he is convinced that one of his greatest life lessons has been to learn how to love unconditionally. He admits that it is a lesson with which he is still struggling. For much of his life, he had the mistaken assumption that happiness could be found in relationships by getting the other person to "think like me." He has come to realize that true love is the ability to perceive other individuals as they are, "with no desire on your part to change them." Even after having come to this realization, however, Ken admits that he has yet to find true intimacy in a one-to-one relationship with a woman, prompting him to say, "There is more to learn."

An example from the Cayce files of an individual positively meeting the consequences of previous actions is the life of Frances Davidson, who was seventeen years old when she obtained a physical reading to help her with a serious weight problem. The reading stated that the problem was a glandular condition and could be corrected with outdoor activity, exercise, and a change in diet that eliminated starches. Additional recommendations included spinal manipulations and the consumption of grape juice throughout the day, mixed half-and-half with water. The treatment was followed, and five months later, her mother reported that Frances had lost a lot of weight and was almost down to her ideal dress size. Because the health reading had proven so helpful, the family requested a life reading for the girl. During the course of her second reading, Cayce traced the glandular imbalance that was causing her predisposition to weight gain to a lifetime in Rome:

> There we find the entity excelled in beauty, in the ability to carry in figure, in body, the games that were a part of the experience.
>
> And too oft did the entity laugh at those less nimble of activity, owing to their heaviness in body.
>
> Hence we find the entity not only meeting same in the present from a physical angle but there are the *necessities* of it being worked out by diet as *well* as outdoor activity. 1339-2

She was encouraged to continue being active in outdoor sports, especially golf, archery, boating, riding, and tennis. By doing so, Frances could meet those same emotions within herself that had led to the weight problem in the present.

Cayce often discussed the idea that our challenges and difficult experiences in life are not so much because of others, but as a means of an individual addressing something within self. A twenty-seven-year-old woman, still living at home and having problems with both her parents and her brother, wanted to know what kind of karmic debt she was working out with these three people. Cayce advised her that there really isn't such a thing as a karmic debt between people, but rather there is a memory within oneself that has the possibility of being worked out by being with certain individuals. The woman's current situation was an opportunity to transform herself by working on these relationships with her family members (1436-3).

Another physical case history of an individual meeting self is the story of Carl Thompson, a twenty-one-year-old student studying to become a physician. His only physical problem seemed to be a tendency toward anemia. He was told that his life could lead to erratic love affairs, to violence, or to the opportunity to make a great deal of money. More than anything else, Carl's free will would play a major role in deciding the course and direction of his life.

The reading told Carl that the anemia would present itself throughout much of his life unless he took measures to address what had caused the problem in the first place. Apparently he had been a warrior in Peru who took part in overthrowing the country's government and leader; in the process "much *blood* was shed." (4248-1) The result of his meeting himself in the present was anemia.

Carl's additional past lives included a sojourn at the time of the Crusades, when he had attended to both the physical and mental problems of people who had been injured. For this service to others, he had gained and continued to possess talents in both anatomy and psychiatry. As an armorbearer in Egypt, he had led a rebellion against the king but had later reconciled with the ruler, and eventually he gained in that lifetime, being able to learn and grow because of the various experiences he had been through. In the present, Carl was encouraged to pursue work as a teacher or as a physician and counseled to give expression to his own development, focusing on a balanced approach that would assist him physically, mentally, and spiritually.

From the perspective of the Cayce readings, it is not that God visits challenges and tribulations upon individuals; rather, it is that each soul is integrally connected to everything that happens in that life. In 1934, Cayce told a forty-year-old sales manager with problems in his business that it was a grievous error to think that God imposes any challenging condition on us for any reason. Instead, such conditions or experiences originate at the level of the soul as a means of correcting imperfections within one's self (257-128). The only thing holding us back from soul development is self.

When a forty-nine-year-old housewife inquired during a reading about her worst fault, Cayce replied, "What is ever the worst fault of each soul? *Self—Self!*" When the woman asked how to overcome this fault of selfishness, the answer came:

> Just as has been given; showing mercy, showing grace, showing peace, longsuffering, brotherly love, kindness—even under the most *trying* circumstances.
>
> For what is the gain if ye love those *only* that love thee? But to bring hope, to bring cheer, to bring joy, yea to bring a smile again to those whose face and heart are bathed in tears and in woe, is but making that divine love *shine—shine*—in thy own soul! 987-4

Sometimes people choose to express this love at a soul level by assisting others with challenges or difficulties that they have overcome themselves. The contemporary story of Gwen provides an illustration. Now in her mid-fifties, she has worked for more than thirty years in the fields of special needs and autism. Gwen described her horrible upbringing:

> I was born to a paranoid, schizophrenic mother who didn't like me or want me. A deaf-mute aunt and my eight-year-old brother were put in charge

of my care. I was isolated, had no socialization, and was totally nonverbal until starting school at age six. I had no self-esteem, was painfully shy, never knew what was normal, appropriate behavior, and was constantly trying to just stay alive in a violent, dangerous environment. Food, clothing, and shelter were never adequate.

When I was eight years old, my brother lied his way into the navy when he was sixteen. My aunt was put away, and I was left to cope with an insane woman by myself . . .

Although the experience was very traumatic, in retrospect Gwen is convinced that her childhood provided her with valuable lessons she has been able to use throughout her life. In addition to her talent at working with special-needs children and adults, in her opinion she has become a stronger person because of these early challenges in life. They also enabled her to learn how people can destroy their own mental health through anger and grudges. Because of her experiences in childhood, "I learned nonverbal, intuitive communication which made me very effective in my work later on."

After she grew up, Gwen was drawn to children and adults with autism. She seemed to identify with them, just as they could identify with her. She understood them in spite of their inability to communicate. Without her childhood upbringing, she would not have been as effective in her work. In part, her work also enabled her to overcome her own insecurities and her feelings of low self-esteem. Interestingly enough, those same insecurities would later be tested when she was nearly paralyzed by arthritis.

After many years in her work, Gwen developed severe arthritis. Rather than being assisted by her numerous medications, the problems multiplied, and she became almost incapacitated with pain. Because so much of her identity was invested in her work, she began to panic. All of the old fears regarding self-esteem and her lack of worth resurfaced. Knowing that she really wouldn't be able to continue her job much longer, she started to fear for her future:

> I could no longer do the job I'd had for twenty-three years. I really needed to give it up but I was afraid to. I thought I was too old, too stupid, too dated, to ever get another job with the salary, benefits, vacation time, etc., that this one offered. The job not only provided financial security but an identity, purpose, lifelong friendships, recognition, etc. At the same time, I was in constant pain. My husband had to help dress me, tie my shoes . . . I slept with five pillows to realign my body nightly; my husband had to cut my food, and I used special adaptive utensils to eat with. My husband said, "Quit!" but he did not understand the depth of my fear and dependency.

Finally, Gwen had a severe allergic reaction to all of the medication she had been given, and she ended up in the hospital emergency room in anaphylactic shock. In desperation, she asked God what she was supposed to do. Should she quit? Should she stay? Although she was very much afraid of giving up the job, she said she was willing to surrender her will to do whatever God wanted. That night she had a dream:

> I was walking on the sandy shore of a desert lake. Far in the distance, a tall figure in a white robe was walking toward me. As we approached each other, I saw it was a bearded man in his thirties. There was no one else present. As he neared me, he smiled

kindly at me and raised his hands up for me to see the scarred nail holes in his palms. While still smiling but not moving his lips in speech, I "heard" in my head the words: "Don't sell my body for thirty pieces of silver, and don't sell yours either."

He turned and walked back the way he had come. I stood and watched him go, with tears on my face, until he was no longer visible.

The next morning Gwen went to the personnel office, applied for retirement, took the four months of sick leave she had saved up, and "never worked there another day."

The change proved to be for the best. Shortly thereafter, Gwen threw away all of her medication and began working with the Edgar Cayce dietary recommendations for arthritis. When she began feeling better, she got a new job. Within nine months, her entire life had improved dramatically: "I cut my own food, used regular utensils, slept without five pillows, and dressed myself. I had a wonderful, fun job with Easter Seals, new friendships, a new purpose, new joy, and none of my fears had manifested."

In summing up her life experiences thus far, Gwen believes that it's important to try to transform whatever comes one's way, seeing the good that might result:

Many times something awful turned out to be the gateway to something wonderful. A crummy job was the stepping-stone to a great job. Divorcing a toad and finding the prince. I loaned money to a friend who became terminally ill and couldn't pay me back. Three months later, after I forgave the debt, I found a hundred-dollar bill by a trash can. I was stuck by the road with a flat tire and subsequently was not involved in a fourteen car-and-truck wreck two miles up the road. I used to take care of a baby who suffered from seizures. He developed pneumonia, and his mother called to tell me that he was probably going to die before morning. He did not die, although it took ten days to turn him around. All the time he was on oxygen, he never had a seizure, which led to the discovery that he had an oxygen apnea problem that had caused the seizures. After three months of oxygen therapy, he never had another seizure. He had to nearly die of pneumonia before he was cured of seizures.

Gwen's philosophy and approach to life are really quite simple: "Look past the dark for the light."

The story of Daryl is one that illustrates how an individual often receives the greatest challenges as well as greatest satisfaction through the same activity. Though he is now retired, music has always been an important part of Daryl's life. Even before starting school, he loved music so much that his mother enrolled him in piano lessons in spite of the fact that money was tight during the Depression. He also met his wife through a musical recital, and the two have long taken part in musical endeavors together. In time, Daryl earned a master's degree in vocal music and pursued advanced study in musical composition. He spent years teaching music in secondary schools and college before retiring.

Although music has been important to him, however, it has also provided him with some of his greatest challenges. Just one of those challenges came in the form of a musical colleague with whom Daryl had studied and who eventually became his boss. There was some measure of rivalry between them that escalated when Daryl composed a musical composition for his boss's brass sextet. That experience had an impact on much of his later career. Daryl recalls the story:

I composed a piece for his brass sextet. There was general agreement that my composition was musically successful, causing him to feel threatened. Later his group performed in a public fanfare which I had written, but he changed the part without my knowledge, ruining the piece and making me furious. I believe this happened through his incompetence rather than from malice. As department chairman, he gave only tepid endorsement of my professional work, preventing me from being promoted, even though I had graduated more and better majors than the rest of the music faculty combined. He made recommendations to downsize the music department, threatening to eliminate my job . . . He then retired [as department chair] and took over the downsized department. At his retirement banquet, I made a stirring speech about what a fine guy he was. My son and family later became his next-door neighbors, so pleasantries were maintained . . .

According to Daryl, experiences such as this one have enabled him to understand the necessity of learning unconditional love and wisdom in his interactions with others. Through his experiences with other people, he has grown as a person. In his opinion, many of his challenges in life might not have occurred if he had then possessed the wisdom that he now has because of going through those events. In addition to learning love and wisdom, Daryl describes his own growth as an individual as changing "from a condition of nearly terminal naiveté to that of a more realistic appreciation of human nature." Soul growth is the result as an individual positively meets life's challenges.

Although Cayce believed that an individual's life experiences were a necessary part of soul development and personal transformation, he warned against looking upon another's problems as something that the person deserved or as simply the fulfillment of some kind of karma. Each individual is worthy of the same measure of love and compassion and of our efforts to provide whatever assistance is possible. The story of a fifty-seven-year-old woman named Louise illustrates this point.

Louise received a life reading and was told that her past incarnations included that of a homemaker in Colonial America who had gained through her dedication to helping create a positive and balanced life for every member of her household. In Egypt, she had also done positive work by helping guide individuals to their best vocation. In an earlier incarnation in Palestine, she had often pursued freedom and liberty. That life experience had led her to a number of individuals suffering from hardships and personal sorrows in their lives. Rather than empathizing with their life challenges, however, Louise had seen their morose behavior as due to their unwillingness to get on with their lives, either because they were hardheaded or short-sighted. For this lack of feeling, she had lost.

During the course of her reading, when Louise inquired about why she had been forced to witness and experience the death of her two sons in the present, Cayce referred to her lack of empathy in the Palestine experience: " ... ye experienced and saw many a mother, many a home lose hope, lose help, lose all, ye are meeting this in thy own experience." (2280-1) She was encouraged to begin working with others who had experienced the same loss as she, enabling her to grow and find peace in the process. Undoubtedly, her life experiences helped her to face and meet the same hardships that she had once been unable to understand.

In terms of soul development, the primary purpose

for an individual to go through this process of meeting self is to provide the soul with present-day circumstances that parallel a previous experience. Although the soul may have lost in a similar situation in the past, in the present a different choice may be made, enabling the individual to learn a valuable lesson in the process. Unfortunately, there are a number of instances in the Cayce files where it appears that the soul repeated the same mistake and failed to learn the lesson. The case of Kitty Howell is one example.

As long as she could remember, Kitty had experienced a difficult relationship with her father. Throughout her childhood, he never seemed to trust her and was always questioning her regarding her activities. That difficulty and the feelings of animosity between them did not diminish as Kitty grew older.

It might appear that this situation was the cause of Kitty's eventual infatuation with an older man. She was twenty; he was forty-three. To make matters worse, the man was also married and happened to be her boss. The two began a love affair, and Kitty felt much guilt over the situation. She claimed she loved the man and wanted to be with him, but he was married. She had been raised in a very religious home, and the experience caused her much inner turmoil. When she wrote Cayce to request a life reading, her letter said: "For months I have felt that I stood at the crossroads, not knowing which road to take or which way to go. I have almost gone completely insane, because this indecision, this not being sure of which is right and which is wrong, is more than the human mind can stand."

As soon as the reading began, Cayce traced the cause of her problem to her most recent incarnation, At that time, she was married to a man who had reincarnated in the present as her father. Although the two had planned to build a home and family together in the earlier life,

Kitty became infatuated with another man. In the present, that individual had returned as her boss. In their most recent past life, the two had also begun an affair, breaking up Kitty's marriage. Obviously, that situation was the cause of her father's mistrust in her.

The reading counseled Kitty that a soul problem she needed to overcome was her frequent giving in to self-indulgence and self-gratification. Cayce asked her to ponder the following regarding her current turmoil: " . . . is this for thy soul development, or for the satisfying, gratifying of the moment? The inner self rebels. *Why* do ye allow self to be so led?" (2960-1) Cayce told her that she possessed real talents as a secretary or as a recorder of statistics and data because of a previous life in Egypt, when she had been a record keeper. Those talents could best be used elsewhere. Her interest in religion was connected to an incarnation at the time of Jesus when Kitty had been associated with some of the holy women and the disciples. She was encouraged to break off the affair and to begin to place some of her energies into focusing upon the needs of others; by doing so, she would soon find the relationship that she sought.

Even after the advice had been given, Kitty asked whether her boss's intentions were sincere toward her; the response was short: "You are just another 'affair.' Will ye accept, will ye reject, the truth?"

According to the reports on file, one of Kitty's aunts stated that her niece tried to break off the affair and was subsequently fired. Rather than being depressed, Kitty mentioned her relief that the whole situation was over. However, the pull between Kitty and her boss eventually won out. A short time later, the two ran off to California together, repeating the same pattern that was supposed to have been overcome in the present. Unfortunately, no follow-up regarding the lives of any of the individuals concerned is on file.

A more positive outcome regarding a soul overcoming a past-life inclination is contained in the account of Abigail Winters. Abigail was born into a family of great wealth and appeared to have everything. Her advantages were short-lived, however, because her father went bankrupt in the 1930s in a four-million-dollar real estate deal. Almost overnight the family went from great wealth and a magnificent home to "illness, poverty, and misery" and a poor hovel that they called home. Although extremely creative and intelligent, Abigail was not a pretty child, by her own admission, subjecting her to much cruelty at school and at home. In fact, home was the source of Abigail's greatest challenge, in the form of her mother.

By all accounts, Abigail's mother did not make a successful transition from wealth to poverty. She had been raised in a 120-room mansion and had married wealth, but was now forced to survive from one day to the next. The stress was taken out on Abigail, who remembers often being told, "You should have never been born," and "You would be better off dead." Those comments were taken to heart, leading Abigail to make six suicide attempts between the ages of eight and fifteen. Perhaps because of her focus on suicide, Abigail often imagined that she had killed herself in a previous life.

Thankfully, at fifteen, Abigail's looks transformed, and she grew into a very attractive young woman. This transformation caused her mother a great deal of jealousy. When boys started asking Abigail out, her mother either put down anyone who showed an interest or asked, "Why would he be interested in you?" When Abigail turned seventeen and her father died, she left home and went through a series of careers as a showgirl, a model, a lounge pianist, and an "extra" in several movies. She had a series of failed relationships, including two divorces. Her life problems caused her again to give a great deal of thought to suicide.

Finally, in the midst of yet another bad relationship, Abigail took too many sleeping pills when her lover informed her that he was seeing an old flame. That night she slipped and fell on a scissors, which became imbedded in her knee. After much bleeding, she passed out and was later found and taken to the hospital. Nearly dead, she was informed that she had severed a nerve in her leg. After a series of operations and complications, including gangrene, her foot turned black and doctors recommended amputation. Abigail just couldn't take any more difficulties. She decided that she would rather be dead than face the amputation. While still in the hospital, she attempted to hang herself in the bathroom, using a strong belt looped over the ceiling's water pipes. After she hung herself, she apparently passed out, because the next thing she remembered was walking through a library:

> I was in a vast, sunlit library, without a ceiling but with a blinding white light coming from above. Shelves of books, five levels in height, stretched into the distance, yet the room seemed circular for I had to stand in the center. I was aware of ancient "monks" in white robes (no hoods) and especially one who looked like Father Time, with a long white beard and I think a rope sash. He rose up to get my book from the third level. I wasn't allowed to see in it, read it, or know its contents.
>
> After reading in it, he closed the book and addressed me. I watched him carefully to see his reaction upon reading so that could clue me a bit on the contents. His expression changed, sobered, and became heavy and sad. He was kind and gentle. He gave me instructions and knowledge telepathically, some of which I only remembered when it came true . . . Aloud, he said one thing, quiet and deep:

"You know that is not the way!"
Oh, yes, I knew that and had forgotten it! I felt stupid and ashamed, though he did not cause me to; it was my own actions I was facing. His kindness told me that he understood my worries. I was given the knowledge that I would be able to keep my foot and that it would soon get well with no limp. I would have twenty years of pain with it, then none. I would have *lots more* turmoil and misery, for which I'd be even more justified to feel suicidal, but that I *must not do it again!* I agreed and promised. [I learned that] this was the last time they'd save me from an attempt, which they had done many times before. Also I'd been a suicide in the life just past. I knew this. I queried, "My memory of jumping out of a window in Natchez on New Year's Eve 1899?" Yes, it was authentic . . .

Shortly after, Abigail found herself conscious again in the hospital bathroom. The belt appeared as though it had been sliced through. Her neck was bruised, torn, and sore but she was alive. The next day her attempt was discovered; that same day she forbade the doctors to amputate her foot.

True to her visionary experience, the color returned to her foot, and it was not amputated. Eventually she was released from the hospital. Just as had been prophesied by the old monk, Abigail's life contained a great many challenges and difficulties. In all, she had three marriages and thirteen engagements. She had problems with bankruptcy, illnesses, relationships, and her mother, who lived to be ninety-six. On the positive side, she had a daughter and gained some prominence as a writer and society columnist. However, her life has not been easy.

Now in her sixties, Abigail is convinced that a lifetime of challenges has been her opportunity to "stick it out" and overcome the suicidal urge that had carried over from her past. Her life experiences have provided her with much opportunity for spiritual growth. She *has* overcome the suicidal urge and has worked through many of her own fears regarding intimacy. She has also continued to work on her resentment toward her mother—by her own admission, a lesson she's only accomplished "seventy-five percent." Although she's overcome much, including the suicidal urge and a variety of fears regarding being broke, homeless, or seriously ill, she considers herself a work still in progress. As long as she's alive, she's convinced that there is more to learn.

What if, like Abigail, each of us were a work in progress? What if each of us were given a personally designed curriculum to help us become all that we were meant to be? What if this curriculum had to be repeated until it was learned? What if everything we sent out came back to us? What if all of our thoughts, words, and actions became the basis for soul lessons and soul strengths that we chose to encounter later on? What if life really were about learning?

Spiritual Growth and Personal Loss

Use hindrances then ever as stepping-stones and not as wraths that would drag thee from thy purpose or from thy ideal.   *1549-1*

What if our losses in life could be seen as much more than personal tragedies, as opportunities for personal growth? What if there were another way of looking at everything that happens to us? What if even something "bad" could eventually be transformed into a positive experience through our own efforts and determination? What if we were not really victims and our losses were not really punishments? Ultimately, what would happen if each of us became a better person for having the opportunity to encounter every experience that came to us in life?

From the perspective of the Cayce readings, individuals constantly draw to themselves experiences and relationships that can ultimately be instrumental in the soul's transformation. When seen this way, even our challenging life experiences can eventually be helpful. An example from the Cayce files is the case of Jim Murray, who was a forty-six-year-old executive with IBM when he decided to obtain a life reading in 1937.

Previously, Jim's five-year-old daughter had been helped by a series of physical readings, enabling the child to overcome a problem with skin discoloration that doctors at the time had called incurable. The girl had suffered from irregular patches of white pigmentation all over her skin (vitiligo), and the readings' treatment had been successful. The readings' success prompted Jim to obtain his own reading and to inquire about his life and the direction in which he could best express his own talents and abilities. He was frustrated at work and felt there was something missing from his life. Always good with money, he was hesitant to simply leave his job for fear that it would adversely affect his family's living situation.

In discussing Jim's past lives and examining what his soul had learned (or failed to learn) in each, Edgar Cayce explored lifetimes in Revolutionary America, the Holy Land, Arabia, and Egypt. Jim was reminded that there were definitely other incarnations that Cayce could have discussed, but that those mentioned were chosen to help Jim understand his current situation and aid his mental and spiritual growth.

The reading discussed the fact that, at a soul level, Jim possessed exceptional abilities in dealing with people. Sensitive to how his activities affected others, he had a strong sense of honor and justice. His ability to assess the talents and weaknesses of other people was acute, and he was warned not to become judgmental in his recognition of another's frailties. More than anything, Jim's reading suggested that his purpose in the present was to become aware of a personal and close relationship with the Divine. According to Cayce, he had attempted this same purpose, and had failed, in an earlier lifetime. Apparently, that was the central ingredient missing from his life.

In tracing Jim's soul history, he had been involved in the early foundation of Washington, D.C., after the Revolutionary War, and was instrumental in helping the new government establish trade agreements and policies. From that lifetime, he possessed abilities in diplomatic service that needed to be put to use in the present. During an incarnation in the Holy Land, Jim had been a wealthy member of the Jewish Sanhedrin. At the time, he had been very rich in worldly goods but had gained spiritually because of the way he dealt with other people. He also had lost in that life, however, because of a tendency to be too indecisive and because he had failed to cultivate his own understanding of spiritual truths, even though the information lay within his reach. In spite of his being a member of the Sanhedrin, he had never really experienced a close and personal connection with the Divine.

His talents for dealing with various peoples had also been cultivated in Arabia at a time when the country was an enormous trade and business center. Jim had served as a banker for commercial exchange among many cultures and countries. He had become adept in activities dealing with finance but had lost spiritually because of his tendency to become too controlling in directing the lives of others. In Egypt, he had both gained and lost. He had gained for his efforts in bringing people together for activities affecting the greater good of the entire country. He had lost when his own reputation prompted him to turn his notoriety into personal power and fame.

Jim was told that he was highly sensitive to the prospect of being dominated by others and the accompanying fear of losing control. Regardless of how his life unfolded, he needed to be at peace and not become resentful or anxious, causing him to make errors in judgment. He was reminded that God was aware of his life and his activities, "For He is mindful of the sparrow. How much more, then, is He mindful of His children, His companions . . . ?" and that one of his most important purposes in the present was to become more aware of his connection to the Creative Forces. Jim was advised to "Love the Lord, keep His ways, manifest them in the every walk of life. Let others do as they may, but as for thee and thy house, *love*, obey, the *living God!*" (1497-1)

In spite of Jim not feeling completely fulfilled in his work, Cayce advised him not to make a change but to let events unfold that would prompt him to find his next calling. These events were predicted to occur within the next three years.

Three months later—much earlier than anticipated—Jim faced an experience that caused him to lose all control over his life. In spite of his position and his years of service with the company, he was deeply troubled when his boss at IBM decided to demote him. Perhaps it was part of the test that would enable Jim to learn to rely on his faith in God. Nonetheless, he wired a telegram to the Cayces, requesting an emergency reading:

> Was informed today I must surrender title and position now held after fourteen years' work and contribution to present business but suggestion made that I might continue in subordinate capacity. (Stop.)
>
> This situation following counsel [in] last reading [it was] not forced by me. (Stop.)
>
> Feel it is impossible for me to accept demotion. (Stop.)

> ... Shall I follow my desires and resign from the
> company ... [?]

Shortly after the telegram was received, a new reading was undertaken. It reminded Jim not to become over-anxious and suggested that the experience he was facing could become a purposeful one. He was advised to follow through on his desire to resign. Since he possessed talents as a consulting engineer, Jim asked about the possibility of becoming a consultant in this field. The reading informed him that that was the proper channel, especially if he focused in the direction of foreign affairs and relationships, helping to forge the bonds of peace between countries through his work as a consultant. As a last bit of advice, the reading stated: "Do not become panicky; do not become overanxious, but let this experience be rather used as stepping-stones to greater opportunities—and never a stumblingblock!" (1497-3)

After receiving the reading, Jim wrote: "I am, with God's help, going to try to follow all that has been revealed—without question." Later reports on file indicate that Jim became a consulting engineer who also patented practical inventions for the home. In spite of his continued focus on work, however, friends noted that there had been a change in his life in that "He has been trying to follow the Law of Love and to walk with God, to exercise patience and carry on in the way set before him."

A contemporary example showing how even a tragic loss can eventually result in a positive outcome is told in Cindy's story. The experience was with her fiancé:

> When I first met Adam, it was an extraordinary connection of someone I had known for eons. There was a love between us with an intensity beyond description. As we were planning a life together, he

died suddenly of a heart attack. In my pain, thoughts of my death or suicide did not seem morbid or unhealthy. I saw no reason to live yet did nothing to end my life.

Cindy recalls going through all of the stages of grief, especially anger. For a time, she often vented this anger at people and events that had no connection to her fiancé's death. Although she eventually married, adopted a daughter, and got on with her life, she never forgot Adam or what he meant to her. In her career as a high school counselor, she was able to use this experience in order to help others who were facing loss or problems with projecting anger onto some unrelated situation. In reflecting back upon the experience, Cindy states:

It was the greatest experiential learning for me. First, I lived through a depth of pain that I never thought I would leave. Secondly, I was strengthened for all of life's trials that followed. And finally, I have been able to help others in my professional life because of this event.

Years later, Cindy had a dream in which Adam came to her and spoke of giving a helping hand. He told her that he had needed to leave, and then the two embraced and kissed. Although she wanted to speak with him longer, it appeared as though there were others he was helping, and he had to go. Cindy awoke from the experience convinced that they had spoken, touched, and kissed. It had been much more than simply a dream.

Another case of loss is contained in the story of Michelle Donovan, a thirty-six-year-old woman who lost her husband, not through death but to another woman. It was the greatest challenge of her life because, in addition to the fact that she didn't even see it coming, she lost everything in one fell swoop: her husband, her home, her security, and her husband's family, with whom she had been close. In order to survive the situation, she moved to another state, also losing her friends and her job in the process. After the move and settling in as best she could, she got a new job and really tried to work on forgiveness. It wasn't easy. She had long talks out loud with God, asking Him why it had happened. She continued to be upset and to feel victimized by the entire situation. The fact that she had lost everything kept coming to her mind.

One day when she was outdoors walking by herself, she felt as if she had had enough. In response, Michelle yelled out, "Okay, God, if all of this shit was to make my life better, show me a sign!" Less than a half mile later, she looked up into the sky and saw *three* rainbows soaring before her! According to Michelle, after that experience, "I thanked God and went on about my new life."

In the intervening years, Michelle has met "a wonderful man," married him, bought and renovated a hundred-year-old house, adopted a slew of dogs and cats, and found a job she loves, doing casework for a U.S. Congressman, a job in which she has the opportunity to help many people. Because of the divorce, she learned forgiveness and also moved beyond the need to control her life. She says, "I don't take things so seriously because I know that God has the master plan, so why sweat it?"

Taking life as it comes is exactly the approach of Robert Evans. At eighty-five, Robert thought he and his wife, Vera, would be enjoying their retirement years together. Unfortunately, for the last six years, she has been completely incapacitated in a nursing home. She had also been treated in a day care center two years previous to that. Vera is a victim of Alzheimer's.

The couple met in 1936 and spent many wonderful years together. After a series of careers as a cook, working for customer relations and training for TWA, serving as a salesman for a variety of companies, and selling life insurance, Robert began working with planning and meetings for a national business organization. It was a position he held until his retirement in 1979. After his retirement, he worked with Vera for more than ten years, helping her with her tole painting classes. As an instructor, Vera often had as many as fifty-five students, and Robert served as the resident carpenter, cutting out designs for the wood.

In addition to tole painting and spending time with their children and grandchildren, the couple loved to travel. Together, they logged more than 84,000 miles in an Air Stream trailer before Vera became ill. As early as 1985, Robert noticed something wrong during a bike ride. After a short ride, Vera ran into the back of his bike, hit her head on the street, and ended up in the hospital for nineteen days. They continued their vacations together until 1992, when Vera's condition no longer permitted travel.

Today, Robert visits his wife twice each day without fail and feeds her lunch and dinner. Her mind has completely deteriorated. She cannot walk or talk. She does not know who he is, nor does she respond to anything that he does or says. She sleeps continually but is placed in a reclining chair each day by 11:00 a.m. and 5:00 p.m. so that Robert can feed her. He says that all of his efforts come from wanting to make certain his wife is taken care of. People often ask him why he spends so much of his time with Vera when she doesn't even know him. Robert's answer is simple: "It's a job, and I've had lots of jobs." More than anything else, however, he says it's "because I love her."

Rather than becoming depressed or feeling burdened by the situation, Robert thinks that the experience has given him the opportunity to put into practice everything he has learned throughout his life. He does not seem to mind taking care of Vera. According to other residents in the nursing home, he is often an example of good cheer and optimism. In addition to caring for his wife, he often checks in on other residents to see how they are doing. Even though his retirement years did not end up the way he once dreamed, Robert still believes his life serves a purpose. In his own words, "I like doing things for other people."

Because of the nature of free will, acquiring a conscious awareness of one's relationship with the Divine is not necessarily something a soul simply achieves and then sets aside in order to move on to the next lesson. The case history of Estelle Atkins, a forty-three-year-old businesswoman involved in the import business, illustrates how even a soul that has attained a highly evolved awareness of spiritual principles must be vigilant in the application of them.

Estelle obtained her life reading in 1936 at the advice of her cousin. She was drawn to international locales, especially Indochina, and her work gave her the opportunity to explore foreign places and people. She was also interested in metaphysics. Yet, in spite of her success and independence, she often suffered from bouts of self-pity and loneliness. She felt that her loneliness was due, in part, to the fact that, throughout her life, she had been stricken with facial paralysis, causing her to feel unattractive.

During the course of Estelle's reading, Cayce traced her slight facial deformity to the misuse of her beauty in two previous existences. She was told that her greatest abilities lay in the fields of writing, teaching, and lecturing. In these areas, she could awaken the consciousness of others to spiritual truths. She was also supersensitive and possessed a keen intuitive sense. The reading suggested that the reason she often experienced doubts or fear was because her body, mind, and soul were rarely in unison with one another. In addition, Estelle's focus on the material things in life had often caused her to lose sight of the reality of spirit all around her. She was reminded "that Life *is* the manifestation of God in motion . . ." (1298-1)

In terms of her soul history, she had been among the early Mound Builders, settling in southern Florida from the Yucatan peninsula. Throughout that experience, she abhorred the way in which those who were mighty and powerful took advantage of those who appeared to be weak and insignificant. The fact that she often found herself in conflict with those in power made her own life often severe and without material rewards, but in terms of soul development, she had gained greatly. From that experience, she had developed an appreciation for the Divine that resided within each individual.

Previously, she had been a member of one of the tribes of Israel and had risen to a place of prominence as a result of her beauty. Because of the various cultures with which her people came in contact, as a soul she had learned tolerance and had become a champion for individuals being able to worship according to the dictates of their own conscience. Much of her work had been with others, helping her people as a whole. At the same time, however, she had developed a deep longing for some personally meaningful life experience beyond just being of service to others. In the present, that prompting caused Estelle to constantly be driven in search of something that she couldn't quite define. Cayce cautioned her against becoming too focused on her self in this regard.

In a portion of Southeast Asia known in Cayce's time as Siam and now known as Cambodia, Estelle had once been a priestess and had allowed herself every extreme in life. Her reading told her that words failed to describe the spiritual beauty she had once experienced. In fact, there had been occasions in that lifetime when she had literally experienced the magnificence of the Creator in everything around her. That same life, however, had been filled with self-indulgence and the frequent satisfaction of every imaginable desire and passion. She was told that she needed to learn the difference between being tolerant of people and of different experiences and being self-indulgent in her pursuit of them.

In providing her with further counsel for her life's direction, Cayce told Estelle to hold fast to the spiritual principles that had once been a part of her soul history. Although she had often misapplied spiritual truths, she also had it within herself to apply them appropriately. She was told to teach, to write, and to live in such a manner that others could see how godliness could become a practical experience in everyday life:

Thou hast gained, thou hast lost, thou hast known the rise of nations, thou hast known the downfall of individual rulers, of individual nations, owing to their misapplication of divine *truth*, divine love, divine law; turning them into self-indulgence, self-glorification.

Thou knowest *innately* the Way. Thou knowest from personal, soul application. Hold *fast* to that which is good. Give—that ye may have—of self . . .

Show thyself lovely, that ye may have love in thine experience. Not as a possession but as a gift to thy fellow man. Show thyself friendly with the unfriendly, that ye may have friends. Not as possessions but rather as that that makes for the greater channel, that there may be the flow of infinite love as thou hast shed upon thy peoples—yea, thy brethren—yea, thy great ones—yea, thy lowly ones; that they, too, may know they have a friend *in* God, within themselves! 1298-1

According to the reports on file, Estelle corresponded a number of times with Edgar Cayce. In 1943, after reading the book, *A Search for God*, which detailed lessons in spiritual growth, she wrote to request additional copies: "Just as my life reading cleared up so many things for me, so does this book. I am going to send one to an acquaintance in California, and wish I could afford to send many, many copies to persons of my acquaintance . . . A thousand thanks for all you have done for me and mine . . . "

She continued to feel drawn to international locales and eventually made some archaeological trips to Cambodia. During the 1950s, she remained interested in the A.R.E. lecture activities in New York. Estelle responded to a 1951 follow-up questionnaire about her readings and wrote that she found the information invaluable, that it had helped her better fulfill her purpose in life, and that she still referred to the information frequently:

> I have tried to help others as Mr. Cayce suggested, opening new vistas to others whenever possible. The reading cleared up many things for me as to the continuity of life—a pattern; showed how *unimportant* one's position and how important one's life in whatever phase, newsboy or king, for growth; gave me courage to keep my chin up without being full of self-pity; and why unselfishness is so vital to one's fulfillment of the earth cycle. Each rereading of my personal reading brings fresh inspiration . . .

She eventually turned to writing, as her reading suggested, and subsequently published a book based on her own life readings and the readings of a few of her closest friends. Before her death in 1969, she even appeared on national television, discussing her experiences with the Cayce work.

Rather than becoming victimized or incapacitated by

life's experiences, people can turn even the most difficult loss around. Wendy Parker is a fifty-year-old district
judge who has been happily married for nearly thirty
years. Without question, she is convinced that the most
difficult experience in her life prompted her to become
a better person. That experience was the horrendous
loss of her daughter five years ago. Since that event, she
says, "The story of my life is divided into two time periods, before Erika died and after she died":

> All time and memories in my life are marked by
> this event. Erika was twenty-two, happy, healthy,
> bright, loving, and full of compassion. She was
> killed in a car crash; her boyfriend who was the
> driver was drunk. At the time, I was a fallen-away
> Catholic, who only went to church on Christmas
> and Easter to please my mother. I did not do a very
> good job of raising my children with much religious
> background . . . Sometimes I even questioned if
> there really was a God. I guess I was full of doubts,
> but never really pondered on these things.
> I guess I would describe myself as average. I had
> both good and bad qualities and didn't really work
> on any of them. Then Erika died and my life—my
> world—fell apart. Nothing has been the same since.
> I was shaken in every fiber of my being. It is very
> hard to put into words how the death of a child af-
> fects a parent. The closest I can describe it is to say
> that I felt that a bomb had blown me up and there
> wasn't enough of me left to pick up and fill a teacup.
> The physical effects of intensive grief are extreme
> and, although I went to work every day, I was in
> emotional shock for about six months. There were
> extreme changes in appetite and sleep patterns; in-
> ability to focus, concentrate, and remember things;
> and a general feeling of illness. Intense grief was

also accompanied by intense depression, which is very hard to overcome. It became a difficult task to just get up out of bed in the morning. Every normal function of life had to be forced, as the desire to die was very strong. It was very hard for me to go on living, and I prayed to die every day . . .

Wendy believes that her spiritual growth really began during the depths of her depression, when she was forced to look for meaning in her life. She joined the Compassionate Friends—a nonprofit, self-help support organization open to all bereaved parents, grandparents, and siblings—and she began searching for her relationship to God. She went back to church, joined the A.R.E., became involved in a spiritual growth study group, and attended many conferences. For the last four-and-one-half years, she has immersed herself in books, courses, lectures, and seminars on spiritual development. In addition, she says, "I have learned how to meditate, studied Buddhism, learned Tai-Chi, and taken courses on hypnosis, psychic development, and dreams." She does volunteer work for a hospice and a suicide-and-crisis line. Wendy believes, "My soul journey began the day Erika died."

Through this difficult process, Wendy has attempted to become a better person. In retrospect, she's aware that, before the tragedy, her life events had tried to teach her a number of lessons, such as love, compassion, understanding, tolerance, and forgiveness. Although she ignored these lessons in the past, she is now embracing them with much determination:

I had a history of not forgiving people and holding a grudge forever. I have also always been so judgmental of people. I tend to always think I am right and have been unwilling to consider someone else's point of view. It was important to me not to be wrong.

What *lesson* I have learned is that I had to forgive this boy for killing my daughter. It had not been in my nature prior to her death to ever forgive anyone. If I felt that a person had wronged me, then I would hold that grudge for the rest of my life. I always realized that this was a bad quality in myself, but I did not do much to change it, as it did not bother me. I had not spoken to several people for years and was content not to resolve my differences with them. Erika's death changed everything in my life.

I came to understand that my daughter loved this boy and that he was basically a good boy who had made a tragic and deadly mistake. I came to know that I had to forgive him. I hadn't [even] forgiven my neighbor, with whom I hadn't spoken in years, and I had to now face the fact that I had to forgive this boy for killing my daughter.

I can't explain how I did it except to say I knew she would have wanted me to forgive him and, since I couldn't tell her how much I loved her, I felt that I could forgive him for both myself and her. I was able to tell him that I forgave him and, when he stood trial for homicide and drunk driving, I prayed to God to help him in whatever way was best for his soul's growth. I put the matter into God's hands, and when the jury came back with a verdict of not guilty to homicide and only the slightest punishment possible for the drunk driving, I accepted it. It was not easy, but I prayed to God to help me through it— and He did.

Since that time, Wendy has gone to a number of people against whom she had held grudges and asked to be forgiven of past mistakes. In this way, at least, her daughter's tragedy has a positive outcome. She is still working on some of her relationship difficulties because she knows it is imperative for her to find a way to resolve her differences. Although she has made great strides with this lesson of forgiveness, she admits: "Sometimes I find it odd that I forgave that boy for killing Erika, but I can't forgive my sister-in-law for things that happened twenty years ago, but I am trying . . . I didn't even want to change this situation. Now I know that I must!"

What if, like Wendy, instead of being victimized by our tragedies, we managed to become transformed and cocreative because of them? What if everything that happened in life had the potential of becoming a purposeful experience? What if some of the things we encountered were ultimately designed for us to be able to assist others in the same situation? What if our goal in life were to become a better person, assisting others in the same process? What if even our personal losses and hardships could become helpful experiences? What if the very lessons we needed in life were drawn to us just as we needed to learn them?

Spiritual Growth Through Life's Experiences

. . . eventually it will be seen that these will be for the better reaction, the better condition, the better experiences for the body, for its physical, its mental, its soul development—if there will be taken advantage of those conditions that come as opportunities and experiences in the associations and relations. 529-1

What if an individual's life were a process of growth rather than an end unto itself? What if the quality of our life experience were integrally connected to our wills and our own perceptions? What if we chose to grow and develop because of life's events, becoming better able to reach out and help others? What if each of us encountered everything that happened to us for a reason? What if life's experiences were purposeful, orderly, and ultimately helpful in nature? What if we didn't have to look for life's lessons because they were destined to find us?

Perhaps more than anything else, the events of her life have enabled Amanda Richards to overcome her feelings of inadequacy, insecurity, and worthlessness. For as long as she can remember, she never felt accepted or loved as a child. She remembers being a good girl, trying to be disciplined, and striving for good grades in school in order to earn her mother's love, "but it was never enough." She was constantly seeking her mother's approval, but it always seemed just out of reach. Because of the friction between the two of them, when Amanda was nineteen, she moved out of the house. Shortly thereafter, she met and fell in love with her husband. True to form, Amanda's mother did not approve of the relationship and refused to come to the wedding.

When Amanda was twenty-five years old, she became pregnant with her first child. A diabetic for most of her life, she had a difficult time during the final stages of her pregnancy. In order to help reduce her stress, the doctors made her quit work and told her to avoid anything that could cause her stress or anxiety. It was then that Amanda's mother chose to tell her that she had been born out of wedlock and that her father was not her biological father; the man who raised her had adopted her as a baby. To make matters worse, Amanda discovered that her mother had long since told her four other brothers and sisters that she had a different father. As a result, Amanda said, "For months, when I looked in the mirror, I didn't know who I was looking at."

At the age of thirty-seven, Amanda developed heart disease and almost died. She didn't know why she was having such a difficult experience. She had to quit her career in commercial advertising and graphic design. She became depressed and felt even more worthless. At the same time, however, she became convinced that her life just had to have a purpose.

In order to overcome her depression, Amanda began receiving massages, "hoping that whatever needed to come out and be released in me would." It was from her massage therapist that she learned about Reiki—a form of energy healing. After one treatment, she decided that it was exactly what she needed for herself. In addition to having regular massages, she began receiving Reiki. In time, she felt well enough to begin learning Reiki for herself. Today, she is a second-degree Reiki practitioner and a part of the healing ministry in her church. She has also opened her own office, giving Reiki treatments to others. Finally, Amanda believes, "I have found my true calling."

In the process, she has also found herself. Because of her experiences with her mother, her illnesses, working with therapy, and her practice of Reiki, she has gained a sense of herself and her own self-worth. She recalls how, during one therapy session when she was discussing her obsessive-compulsive housekeeping behavior, she told the therapist how she needed to perform a daily cleaning ritual. When her therapist mentioned that she might be trying to make herself feel better by cleaning up what was around her, Amanda had an "ah-hah" experience and realized that she was taking part in the behavior because she felt dirty and worthless about herself.

Rather than being frustrated or angry about the past, she realizes that her life experiences have enabled her to become the person that she is today. No longer feeling worthless or insignificant, she looks forward to sharing her talents with others. Amanda has been able to move far beyond her old thoughts and insecurities about herself:

In terms of my soul growth, something that I've overcome is my feeling of inadequacy. This is a relatively new revelation for me and one that I am now enjoying since I've been on my healing journey. I can't say exactly how I've accomplished this; it's as if a sheet has been pulled away from a movie screen and the answer was revealed on the screen itself... I have learned that I cannot receive validation of my worth from my mother (or anyone else) but that it must come from within myself. I guess I never felt worthy of love before or I felt unlovable, but since my illness I now know how wonderfully I am made in the image of our Creator and that He knows how truly special I am.

In another example of growing through life's challenges, Tammy Barnes said that although she lost a great friend, her husband, to death, she gained immensely in spiritual growth because of the experience. When they had been married for twenty-five years, her husband was diagnosed with a brain tumor and given just months to live. The announcement was not one that Tammy had been prepared for in her sheltered religious upbringing. Overnight, she was forced to become her husband's primary caregiver.

Tammy credits much of her ability to handle the situation to her husband's positive outlook and good nature. Without his encouragement, she admits: "I would have folded and not been able to withstand the situation." Still, taking care of an adult, with no nursing training, proved to be a difficult proposition. Often throughout her husband's illness, she found herself talking to God, simply to ask for His assistance. In addition to being able to continue her work with her husband, those long conversations made Tammy feel even closer to God. Still, at one point, she found herself at her "wits' end." She told God, "You say You only give us what we can handle, but I can't take any more." Suddenly, Tammy's husband called out for her to come and assist him:

He was in the bathroom and had had "an accident" in his pants. He said, "I think I made a mess." It struck me funny, and we both laughed so much, but it sure felt good. Later, after getting him back to bed, I told God: "Okay, I guess I can still take some more. Thanks for the help."

To be sure, after her husband died, Tammy went through a great deal of personal grief. As if in answer to her need for something spiritually uplifting, one day in church about five months after the death, the minister based his sermon on a passage from Romans 5:3-4 that she found especially helpful: "Rejoice in our sufferings . . . suffering produces perseverance, perseverance character, and character hope . . . "

In time, Tammy married again and eventually found herself the primary caregiver for a disabled father-in-law. "Right then I knew why I had needed to learn the caretaker job so well," she said. Although her father-in-law had been given only six months to live, Tammy wouldn't accept it. She had lost her own father more than ten years previously, and she really wanted to have a relationship with her husband's father. Her dedication to him paid off, and he lived for sixteen months. Tammy recalls: "We had many good months to become close friends."

In a very real sense, Tammy believes that her life's events were not problems but learning experiences. In part, they enabled her to overcome a lack of confidence in herself. In addition to becoming stronger in character, she also believes that she has been able to grow spiritually. Although she has learned a great deal, she adds, "I still have much more to gain in life's lessons . . . I just hope I don't lose out on the opportunity."

In recalling his own soul development, Bernard Grant, a sixty-three-year-old artist and retired physician, believes that his greatest progress has come in his ability to express his feelings and to open up emotionally: "In my family, talking about feelings, expressing sadness, or asking for help or cooperation on a project were all forbidden." He remembers that when his father's mother broke her hip and moved in with the family to be taken care of, nobody talked about the stress even though it was evident. When his grandmother died, no one ever talked about it. These types of experiences molded the way in which he dealt with his own emotions.

In 1957, before completing medical school, Bernard and a young woman he knew had sexual relations and conceived a child. The woman went to Detroit to a home for unwed mothers. She called two days after his daughter's birth, and Bernard recalls that he hardly spoke to her: "My mother was in the room, and I didn't want her to know about this . . . [I] totally mishandled it all." The child was put up for adoption, and Bernard and the young woman did not see each other again. The following year, Bernard married and, with the exception of his wife, he never spoke to anyone about the pregnancy, the delivery, or the adoption.

Since that time, Bernard believes that his wife has been instrumental in helping him to become a better person:

> She has been a tremendous source of support, inspiration, and love in my life. I have learned how to express love better, how to accept love, how to compromise, and how to provide support for another person. I tell people that the day I met her was "the luckiest day of my life."

Bernard also credits much of his personal growth to therapy, reading, learning to talk with others, praying and meditating, and expressing himself through painting.

After Bernard retired, it was with his wife's encouragement that he decided to address and heal the situation that he had long neglected. He still felt terrible about abandoning a child he had conceived, and he felt a great deal of guilt because of neglecting the mother at the time of her pregnancy and delivery. As a result, he eventually contacted her, and the two began to search for the daughter they had given up for adoption. In 1996, Bernard got to meet the child he had fathered as a young man, and since that time, they continue to talk on the phone about once a month. The entire experience has been life-changing in enabling Bernard to overcome his inability to express his emotions. He adds, "I feel I've gained some wisdom, become way less judgmental, more patient in many ways, and I've learned to experience and express grief somewhat better."

Another case illustrating how individuals can grow through family relationships is the story of Peggy, a woman in her sixties with four grown children. Now a grandmother, she reflects with a smile on the years when her own children were at home: "The only thing I ever wanted to be was a mother. Somehow, I always knew I was going to be the mother of four children." Given that raising children includes carpools, packing lunches, football games, Girl Scouts, visits to the orthodontist, homework, parent-teacher meetings, scraped knees, slumber parties, driving lessons, and innumerable other challenges, Peggy is convinced that having children has got to be one of the most effective ways an individual can work at soul development.

From her perspective, children have a way of helping to reshape priorities. She's certain that she became less self-centered and more selfless. With four children, Peggy also found herself becoming adept at seeing more than one side of an issue. She also had to become vulnerable and trusting as a parent: "You can't watch your children twenty-four hours a day." It was inevitable that her faith had to grow along with her children. When asked what she has learned as a mother and now as a grandmother, Peggy is quick to answer:

> With age really do come wisdom and patience. You really know you've learned patience when you get grandchildren. I have said to many people that I *thought* I was a good mother, but I *know* I am a great grandmother. If we could only learn to be as loving as parents as we finally learn to be as grandparents, then this world would truly be a wondrous place in which to live.

Of all the things that her family has taught her, Helen Murphy believes the three that stand out the most are forgiveness, unconditional love, and the ability to lighten up when others don't do things exactly her way. Now in her seventies, Helen and her husband, Bob, have been married for fifty years and have raised four grown sons. They have also had their share of challenges, which they have worked through, somehow becoming stronger in the process.

For the first fifteen years of their marriage, the issue was money. There was never enough. If they couldn't pay cash, it wasn't bought. Going out to dinner was almost unheard of—all meals were made from scratch and supplemented by a large garden. Helen often made her boys' clothes and sewed everything from drapes to slipcovers. She also cut her sons' hair until they left home. For years, they couldn't even afford a regular set of dishes and instead used a set of institutional plastic that had been given to them by a relative. The experience taught Helen to be frugal, disciplined, a skilled planner, and a thorough record keeper.

In addition to their problems with money, the couple's

children provided them with some of their biggest challenges and opportunities for personal growth. Their son, William, seemed to provide them with more than his fair share. Although he was charming, social, and loving, he was also irresponsible. Later, the couple discovered he was experimenting with drugs. He also dropped out of college in his sophomore year. At nineteen, William announced that he was gay. Helen asked him how long he had known and, when he said since about the age of eight, she was heartbroken for him: "How sad and lonely he must have been to hide it all those years!"

Bob's acceptance of his son's homosexuality, however, was a bigger hurdle for him to face. He calls the experience his "most trying lesson":

> Having been in the navy for over three years left me with a profound dislike of homosexuals. While on shore patrol duty, I had to patrol some gay bars in San Francisco, and I was repulsed by the behavior I saw.

As trying as it may have been, their son's announcement of his homosexuality was not the final challenge. William began having serious financial problems. Their son defaulted on a loan that the couple had cosigned, resulting in their having to pay it off. Later, he needed money when his bike was stolen. Then he injured his knee water skiing, and Helen and Bob had to cover for the surgery. The list went on and on and eventually totaled many thousands of dollars. Finally, when William was twenty-four, he called them with the news that he had AIDS. Before the couple could even begin to deal with the news, William then tried to commit suicide by taking an overdose of sleeping pills. Bob and Helen went to his aid and took care of him until he decided to stay with friends.

By this time, Bob had learned an important lesson. "I came to see that my son was still my son and that I could be of great service to him by supporting him—unconditionally." The couple became involved in a local AIDS awareness project. With their son's approval, they appeared on a call-in radio talk show on the subject of homosexuality and on a TV program where they were the only parents allowing their faces to be viewed. "We felt it an important statement to show that we didn't feel a need to be ashamed," they said. They were prepared to face any negative feedback; instead, all of their friends and co-workers were extremely supportive. By the time William finally died, the couple felt that they had tried to do their very best.

Now in their retirement years, Helen and Bob often find themselves a source of encouragement and joy to their friends and relatives. They have managed to help different members of their family through their own challenges, striving to be nonjudgmental and supportive in whatever ways they can. The couple's own growth has been prompted by personal experience, faith, volunteer work, spiritual study groups, and eight years in a marriage encounter group. For Bob, the marriage encounter group was "one of the greatest growing together experiences we've ever had." In terms of her own soul development, Helen says, "I still have work to do, but I think I'm making progress."

At sixty years old, Jamie Yates states philosophically that she has discovered "a hard life is not necessarily a bad one, and digging for gold is not easy either." Because of her early upbringing, her greatest challenge in life has been to relearn how to express her feelings. Her mother was extremely strict and a heavy drinker. That combination led to many traumatic experiences with punishment and discipline. Jamie says, "I reached the point at which I refused to cry when being punished, spanked, slapped, etc. Hiding my feelings became easier and easier."

In addition to holding anger against her mother, this dysfunctional relationship led Jamie to problems with trusting and opening up to others. In spite of eventually marrying and having a family, in retrospect, she knows that she isolated herself emotionally from those closest to her and often took medication simply to survive being overwhelmed. When asked how she overcame her emotional dysfunction, she credits bodywork, therapy, and yoga. She also believes that her experiences with Toastmasters have been extremely helpful for building self-esteem, being able to open up and meet others, and learning how to share her ideas.

By going through her childhood experiences and then trying to heal them as an adult, Jamie feels that she has become infinitely more aware of the feelings of others. By learning to express her own feelings, she learned how to sense the needs of others. She also began to express much more of her potential and to become aware of her connection to *spirit*. Yet Jamie is very much aware that her spiritual and personal growth have been a constant process:

> I have a stubborn streak, an old friend that hangs on to old ideas, old hang-ups, old opinions, old prejudices, old tapes. I long for comfort, security, and all the things which make life fun. But I know I must get out of my comfort zone to grow . . . The challenge of a relationship will always bring me lessons because relationships are dynamic, not static. And trust must be earned, not taken for granted. And feelings make us vulnerable.

Convinced that she will always be tested by her old habit patterns, Jamie now sees her life experiences and personal challenges as the tools for her own growth and development: "My light must learn to shine just as brightly as my soul can handle."

In the case of thirty-year-old Angie, one of the most transformative experiences she ever had came as the result of a simple conversation with her father. Like many other people, Angie had her share of difficulties with her parents. Most often, it seemed as if she were completely different than either of them and that there was very little the three had in common. "Normal" conversations with her parents just didn't seem to be a part of their relationship dynamic. Even as an adult, she often felt as though her main interaction with her father was learning how to stick up for herself. A change came in their relationship when her father's mother died.

Angie and her father ended up driving together to the funeral. Her father used the experience as an opportunity to talk about his own childhood. Later, the two drove through the neighborhood in which he had grown up so that he could share some of his memories with his daughter. To her amazement, Angie was surprised just how much she and her father actually had in common: "I heard a lot of myself when he spoke." For the first time, she felt as if she really got to know him—and she learned more about herself in the process. Angie says, "I learned my father was human like the rest of us." That one experience led to a whole new appreciation of her relationship with her family.

Jackie Jones is a fifty-year-old woman who has struggled with feelings of abandonment all her life. Her parents separated when she was about three, and Jackie can recall often feeling as though she had been forgotten and neglected "by someone to whom I should have been very important." Those feelings of abandonment resurfaced after her marriage to and then divorce from her husband of only two years. In the present, it continues to be a challenge because her current husband of twenty-six years is an alcoholic. His problem continues to ignite her feelings of abandonment and neglect, and Jackie says that these experiences have tended to make her "feel insignificant to the people to whom I belong."

Although she was raised in a Catholic home and was familiar with some metaphysical books, her own challenges and the commitments of raising three children, kept her interest in spirituality from blossoming until her mother's death. Always close to her mother, the death was a traumatic experience for Jackie, but it also became one of the most beautiful and moving moments of her life:

> My sister and I spent four days in the hospital with my mother at the time she passed away and spent hours talking about her dying. Mom was in a coma, but opened her eyes at one point. During this period, I felt a heightened sense of connection with spirituality since I knew her death was imminent. On the evening Mom died, about an hour before, my sister and I were talking when I saw a column of brilliant lights, like fireworks with pink, green, silver, and gold—just brilliant! My sister didn't see it. We returned to Mom's bedside and, within the hour, she took her last breath. She had been totally comatose, but with labored breathing and an uncomfortable grimace on her face. Then there was silence and she smiled, nodded her head, and was gone . . . I was blessed to have experienced this.

Shortly thereafter, Jackie's husband lost his job. Because he had been the sole supporter of the family, the situation proved to be extremely difficult and anxiety provoking. However, because of circumstances in the family, Jackie became eligible for a grant to attend the local community college. Shortly after, she got a job in the hospital and received more on-the-job training as a technician. Now she is the primary support for her family, and she's working in a field she loves and in a job she couldn't have imagined several years ago.

Grateful for some of the challenges that have come her way, Jackie realizes that her own fears and insecurities have been helpful in enabling her to assist some of the hospital patients in her care. She declares that her work has become one of the most meaningful experiences in her life: "I have lots of opportunities to interact with patients who are very sick, scared, and in pain. Occasionally, one of them acknowledges the comfort they receive from my words or my touch, and that is very gratifying to me emotionally." She has also formed extremely close relationships with her three children and is grateful for the open communication and interaction that exist among them.

Life's experiences have taught her compassion, tolerance, and the importance of using her will to help shape the direction of her life rather than allowing her fears or the strong will of others to shape it for her. Although she still struggles with her husband's alcoholism, she knows it is something that he has to choose to change, not a change she can force upon him. In a very real sense, Jackie says, "I've gained some sense of purpose in my development and in my relationships with others. I also have a better grasp of what it is that *I'm* responsible for, as opposed to what *others* are responsible for."

At sixty-nine years old, Patrick McGinnis has also had his share of life challenges and opportunities. Very shy and self-conscious as a child, he has had a lifetime of psychological and spiritual growth experiences that have largely left these characteristics behind him. In looking back at his life, Patrick believes that personal transformation has been an integral and important part of his life's journey.

One of his most life-changing experiences occurred in college. Troubled with a serious eye condition that threatened his sight, he was drawn to share his situation with a friend at school. That confidence led his friend to introduce Patrick to a psychic healer. When the healer proved extremely helpful and the condition was healed, Patrick became interested in the psychic and spiritual world. The eye problem and healing sent him on a spiritual quest that has continued to this day.

After his marriage, his younger daughter presented some of the most trying emotional challenges that Patrick and his wife would ever experience as parents. Those challenges culminated in her running away from home at the age of fourteen. While she was gone, in addition to being extremely worried about her safety, Patrick bombarded himself with a barrage of questions: "Did I fail to give her enough discipline?" "Did I give her improper guidance along the way?" "Did I neglect her while she was growing up?" "Am I a failure as a parent?" Those questions and more ran through his mind.

There was a period when the couple felt helpless and totally vulnerable. By his own admission, one of the most important things Patrick had to learn was about letting go. He also had to learn a great deal about forgiveness—both toward his daughter and toward himself. He had to learn to forgive his daughter for what she had done to the family, and he had to forgive himself for all the things that might have caused the situation in the first place.

With the help of friends and a great deal of support from their church and a spiritual support group, the couple managed to survive a horrible period of uncertainty. He also found a great deal of stability through the practice of prayer, meditation, and dream work—tools for inner guidance that serve him even now. Somehow, the couple managed to live through a very trying time. When their daughter returned, they also survived and had to work through a challenging transition period. Now in her late thirties, his daughter has fully reconciled with the family, and all the teen issues have been resolved.

Another serious challenge faced the family when Patrick's job was terminated through a company merger. That experience began a series of financial challenges that he has had to deal with for more than a decade:

> I have had to try several approaches to reestablish financial stability in my 50s and 60s, when I might have been thinking about retiring. Again, prayer and meditation have been essential, but far from infallible. Much learning has come from being willing to try new things, not all of which worked out favorably, and to accept this as part of the growth process.

In personal relationships, he has attempted to be responsive to the need to change and to do things differently: "On several occasions when inappropriate behavior has been pointed out to me, I have been willing to change it simply by deciding to do so. It has been a matter of recognizing the fault, stopping the excuses, and deciding to change."

Moving beyond his past as a shy introverted person, today Patrick frequently finds himself placed in leadership positions. He has accepted those experiences as a challenge to become more sensitive to people's needs and more assertive in helping to bridge differences of opinion that often arise among various personalities. Thankful for a lifetime of learning experiences, Patrick believes he is a more spiritual person because of life's events:

> I have certainly gained in a sense of oneness with

God, which has greatly enhanced my self-confidence, leadership abilities, and other positive traits.
I have also gained in my basic ability to trust in a
higher power, letting go many anxieties and fears.
On the negative side, I sometimes become impatient with others who do not quickly grasp the
truths that are so obvious to me.

Rather than becoming frustrated that he still has more
to learn, he says simply, "I work on rectifying such situations and asking God for forgiveness." Still very much
looking forward to the future, Patrick says that, even
now, he is thankful to have the opportunity to increase
his reliance on his spiritual resources and to continue to
grow in meeting the challenges that life has to offer.

Although Darlene was miserable and had grown to
despise her life over a number of years, it wasn't until age
forty-eight that she finally decided to do something
about it. Alone, staring up at a mountain peak in
Yosemite National Park, she yelled out, "God, I am not
happy!" She hated her job as a graphic artist; she hated
her marriage of nine years; and by Darlene's account,
"Most of all, I hated myself." Long interested in Native
American cultures and realizing that an important ancient truth from many traditions was to simply "Know
thyself," she has since spent a great deal of time trying to
do just that.

In looking back on her life, Darlene can see that a
number of difficult personal relationships tried to assist
her, from a soul level, in developing the sense of self-esteem that she lacked. She had a father who tried to do
everything he could to discourage her from being an artist. "You'll starve as an artist, and you'll be a bum!" he
said. She has had a verbally abusive relationship with her
daughter ever since the child was old enough to think
for herself, and she has had a variety of challenges with

men. Although she finally came to realize that people often act as mirrors to one another—reflecting back those parts of themselves that they do not like—it was only recently that Darlene came to a realization that was truly transforming: "I know that I cannot ever love another human person until I first love the human part of me. " She adds:

> I need to remind myself that Darlene is the human form I have chosen in this lifetime, but that physical body called Darlene is not who I am as a spiritual being. And the physical body I call father or husband is not who they are on a spiritual level! And I forget, sometimes, to love them, especially when I am not having an "I love you, Darlene" day!
>
> Out of my many revolutions have come many revelations. My greatest truth has become that, just because my life sucks, I need to stop blaming other people. And because their life sucks, I will not accept personal responsibility for their illusions of misery. I am taking back my personal power—finally!

Having taken back the responsibility for her life, Darlene is very much looking forward to the rest of her life journey and to all the opportunities and learning experiences that are before her.

A final example of how life's experiences can lead to personal and spiritual growth is the story of Shelly DeAngelo. In spite of the fact that Shelly is in her seventies and has faced a lifetime of challenges, she appears years younger and possesses a warmth and optimism that most people who haven't endured a fraction of her hardships might find hard to come by. However, in spite of her youthful appearance, even from the beginning, Shelly's life was one of hardship:

I was born in 1926 to a young couple who had two-year-old twin girls. My conception and birth were not a joyous occasion because the family was already burdened financially, and the care of the two toddlers was, in itself, a heavy responsibility for my young mother. Unfortunately, since this was before the time when contraceptives were available, married women had little say as to the number of children they would bear or how they would be spaced. But there was *one* small margin of choice available to women—abstinence from sexual relations altogether, and this was the decision that my mother chose.

Her mother's choice led to her father becoming interested in another woman and leaving the family. Because he eventually fathered twelve additional children with his new wife, her father did not contribute financially or emotionally to her upbringing. When Shelly was four years old, she was farmed out to an aunt who lacked both children and mothering skills. It was a situation Shelly would have to live with until she was fifteen.

Perhaps in part because of her upbringing, Shelly completely lacked self-confidence and self-esteem. Although such feelings are not unusual for teenagers, her problems seemed extreme. Her face would turn red when others even looked at her. She was also quiet and withdrawn and not appreciated for her talents. During her senior year, she won first prize in an American Legion essay contest on "How to Help the War Effort." After she was awarded a savings bond at a school assembly, some of her classmates chided her. "Who wrote that for you?" they asked. Her personal image was dealt a further blow when, just prior to graduation, her homeroom teacher announced aloud to the class what each student's future appeared to be. When she came to Shelly, she said,

"You're a sweet girl. The best thing for you is to marry and have a lot of children."

In 1948, Shelly met and married her husband, Hank, who was thirteen years her senior. He was bright, energetic, and ambitious. Unfortunately, he was also extremely authoritarian in raising the couple's four children. That approach led to a great deal of friction in their marriage. Her oldest son was also born with lung problems and developed frequent pneumonia. After a serious bout with appendicitis and subsequent gangrene, it appeared that her son would die. One day while he was asleep in his hospital bed, she stood next to him holding his hand and crying. Suddenly she heard a clear but soft voice over her shoulder say, "It's only a body." There was no one around when she turned to look, but it came to her that even if her son died, his earthly life would be over but it would certainly not be the end of him. The remark put things back into perspective. Shelly squeezed his hand, and he awoke. She spoke about how much everyone missed him. Eventually, the boy recovered.

In addition to the trials of having a home and family, her next major challenge occurred when she returned to college to earn her master's degree to become a rehabilitation counselor. Although it was difficult to be a wife and mother, go back to school, and work part-time to help support the family, Shelly managed to do it. She finished her degree at age fifty-two. Unfortunately, although she interviewed for many jobs, she was passed over for younger graduates. She never was able to work in her chosen field, so she threw her efforts into writing a book, which she completed, only to have it rejected by numerous publishers.

Because she longed for some additional fulfillment in life, she decided to serve as a volunteer. Shelly began working in two mental health facilities. She found the work demanding and engaging. However, because she spent so much time away from home, Hank grew lonely and began participating in ballroom dancing at the local senior center. That led to his infatuation with several good-looking widows at the center. The experience further humiliated Shelly and greatly challenged her insecurities and her fear of abandonment.

The family was thrown into its greatest challenge, however, because of Shelly's youngest daughter. While she was at graduate school, a man climbed through her window, took a knife, stuffed a sock in her mouth, and raped her. He threatened to kill her if she ever told anyone. The girl's attacker was never found. In spite of receiving counseling and some psychotropic medication to help her with the trauma, Shelly's daughter eventually dropped out of school. She began to hallucinate and think that she was being stalked. Approximately one year after the rape, she shot and killed a radio disc jockey, convinced that the man had been after her. The crime caused the entire family to be treated like criminals. Because the young man had been very popular in the community, the case had a high profile, and newspaper headlines were frequent. The media hounded the family at every opportunity. Eventually, Shelly's daughter was released to a mental health facility, where she lived until being released back to the family.

Another challenge occurred when Hank suffered a stroke and could no longer speak or walk without assistance. For more than a year, Shelly cared for him in their home as one would care for an infant. Although his body was almost completely destroyed by the stroke, his mind remained very active. The situation caused him a great deal of personal frustration, and Shelly did what she could to help him:

   I took him for rides in the car regularly and to visit friends and to watch the ballroom dances that he had enjoyed so much. And I helped him to maintain a sense of humor during this time. He always responded warmly to me, often just patting my hand or pulling me with his strong left arm toward his face so that I would kiss him. We had a new level of companionship that was trying for both of us, yet one in which the two of us who had been together for so long (just short of fifty years) rose to a new level of bonding. He could manage to say single words, and I was touched one time when I asked, "How are you feeling today?" and he responded, "Lonesome." Here was the strong Aries who had participated in community politics, was active in several groups, served in leadership capacities, was a successful author, and enjoyed people, yet now he was locked in his own body. I learned from him how souls can endure with a quiet courage and manifest dignity and nobleness, even in demeaning circumstances. His strong Aries disposition was softened due to this experience, and my Libran softness, on the other hand, was toughened.

After her husband's death, she moved to another state in order to help a ninety-year-old uncle who was ill. She stayed with him, helping him put everything in order, until he died as well. Shelly considers even that opportunity a learning experience and feels privileged to have had the chance to be with him.

Because of a lifetime of challenges, she admits that there have been occasions when she has felt like a failure: She was an unwanted child; her husband sought out other women; her child was guilty of a horrendous act; she was never able to put her degree into practice; her writing came to naught. However, Shelly also says that she has learned to appreciate all of her blessings. She also believes that she has discovered the root cause of many of her challenges: She remembers committing suicide in another life and leaving a small child who had a very difficult life because of Shelly's act of selfishness and abandonment. She says that, as a result, this current lifetime has given her "many opportunities to be supportive of others and to put their needs above my own":

   I finally realized that all of the difficulties that have occurred to me in this life were not due to my mother or my environment or anyone else. I had to emotionally feel the experience of being abandoned to understand what this involves in a person's whole life. I [also] sense that, in the distant past, there was some self-aggrandizement on my part; I believe that I thought too highly of myself because of some position or rank that went to my head. I have had many demeaning experiences . . . in this sojourn that have offset that notion.

In terms of what she is still learning, Shelly says that, as she grows older, she realizes how precious time really is and how much time she has probably wasted. She wants to learn how to make better use of what time she has remaining: "I still waste time on things that have no lasting importance. The world is not better because I painted the living room!"

What if, like Shelly, we learned to take complete responsibility for our lives? What if we discovered that everyone in our life was there to enable us to somehow become a better person, through love, through challenge, or through both? What if we became aware of the fact that all individuals have something to teach, just as everyone has something to learn, provided they choose to do so? What if we began to see all of life's challenges as our self-selected opportunities for spiritual growth and development? What if we suddenly realized that we haven't simply been handed our life's events and experiences, but instead have reached out for them?

The Nature
of the
Human
Will

And man, through the will, makes for his development or retardment through what he does about that he sees manifested in the material world.   262-56

What if an individual's spiritual growth were predicated not so much upon what happened in her or his life but, rather, on how that individual dealt with what happened? What if it were our perceptions that created and shaped the attitude with which we face life's experiences rather than the difficulty or ease of those experiences themselves? What if free will weren't so much the deciding factor in *what* an individual chose to learn but were, instead, only the determinant in *when* that lesson would be learned? What if, ultimately, the human will were the single strongest factor in determining the success or failure of a person's life?

Repeatedly, the Edgar Cayce readings advised people that the course of their life experiences would be inextricably connected to their personal wills. Although certain probabilities might be inevitable in life, the way in which an individual responded to those probabilities would determine the outcome in any particular situation. For example, a twenty-eight-year-old student, studying for his Ph.D. in history and art, was told in 1936 that the way his life would unfold depended upon how he used his will and the opportunities that came to him. He was encouraged to continue to cultivate the patience and understanding that he had demonstrated toward himself and others in his most recent incarnation as a settler in Michigan. At that time, he had been a champion of peace, hope, and cooperation among the various European settlers and the Native Americans. However, during the same incarnation, he had also experienced poverty. For that reason, he was driven to acquire material resources. Cayce reminded him to keep his priorities in order and to understand that material gains were best achieved through an activity of service to others. The choices he made as he faced this desire to overcome poverty while drawing upon his longing for peace and cooperation among people would help to determine the direction of his life in the present (1173-4).

In the Cayce cosmology, the best use of the human will is not simply to experience the dynamics of freedom of choice but rather to use the will in an optimal manner for personal soul development. The will can be directed in both positive and negative channels. For example, a twenty-year-old student was advised that, with humanity's capacity for free will, an individual either becomes a "co-worker" with God in attempting to bring love into the earth or inadvertently acts as a "stumblingblock" to that very same purpose (2549-1). For that reason, each lifetime ultimately provides an opportunity to serve only self or to act as a channel of blessings and aid to others. Along the same lines, another young man was told that "To make the will one with the Creative Energy should be the desire of *every* being." (78-3) In another instance, a thirty-six-year-old attorney was advised that an individual's ability to take stock of self and then apply the will in the appropriate direction is essentially what determines whether a soul progresses or regresses in any given lifetime (5-2).

One challenge in trying to understand the nature of free will is the misperception that to truly have freedom of choice, our wills must be very different from God's will. An alternative explanation is contained in the readings' discussion of the difference between an individual's *personality* and *individuality*. From the readings' perspective, the personality is essentially the front or the mask we present to the world—most often, it is not who we really are. The personality often changes, depending upon the activity with which we are involved or the people with whom we are interacting. For example, we might present a different aspect of our personality to our loved ones, to our co-workers, or to people we meet only socially. On the other hand, the individuality is our true self. Ultimately, it is who we really are, apart from such things as our fears, our biases, or our desires for the future. It is that part of us that has been consistent throughout our soul history.

With this in mind, the personality self is often prone to exercising the will and making choices and decisions based upon impulses, desires, and habitual modes of behavior. However, the individuality self is much more in alignment with one's soul nature. This true self can exercise the will in directions that ultimately create the greatest good in any given situation. Although we may not always be conscious of this fact, God's will for our lives aligns with the same choices that would be made by our individuality self if only we were able to get our personality self out of the way. Along these lines, Cayce told a fifty-year-old housewife, "As to whether the experience becomes for developments or retardments depends upon which choice is made; whether the experience is to be for constructive building or for the gratifying . . . of the ego of self." (1530-1)

The ramifications of making choices with either the personality self or the individuality self is that only the latter can be assured of leading toward that which is best from a soul perspective. One woman was told that because of her free will and the choices she would make, there could be "no middle ground." (339-1) Either she would lead a very successful and positive life, or she would be unhappy and a complete failure. The likelihood of each of these extremes was dependent upon her will and the spiritual ideals and focus with which she chose to work.

The woman was advised that, because of her soul history, certain experiences were destined to express themselves in her life. It was how she chose to deal with those experiences that would determine her ultimate success or failure. An artist in the present, she had talents that had been previously employed to help others—in one incarnation as an interior decorator and in another as a sculptress—using art to awaken individuals to spiritual truths. However, on other occasions that same talent was used primarily for self-indulgence and personal material gain. In this life, the woman would have to encounter experiences in which she met all of these conditions. Her response to each of these situations would be the determining factor in what came to her.

Emphasizing the importance of one's will in the present, a 1941 life reading for a sixty-five-year-old woman stated: " . . . the entity should understand, no urge, no influence exceeds the *will* of the entity . . . " She

was advised to realize that every choice she made had
an effect upon every aspect of her life. Cayce continued
by saying:

> For, like begets like in every phase of material,
> mental and spiritual experience.
> For, as in the material world ye find that ye do not
> gather figs from thistles, neither in the mental world
> may one think hate and find love in one's bosom;
> neither in the spiritual realm may one entertain the
> desire for ego to express irrespective of others and
> find the beauty of the spiritual thinking life. 2560-1

To be sure, past-life influences were having an effect
upon her current experience, but she needed to keep in
mind the importance of her own will and her choices in
the present because "in spirit there is no time but now."
The importance that the human will plays in determining how we choose to respond to life's situations
cannot be overstated. A case from the Cayce files con-
cerns a thirty-nine-year-old woman named Nancy who
went to Edgar Cayce because of a nonmalignant uterine
tumor. Doctors did not want to perform surgery because
of a serious blood condition. A number of physical readings were given to her between 1930 and 1933. In addition to the physical suggestions for her treatment,
Nancy's reading advised that the tumor had manifested
because of her anger and resentment over the death of
her infant son. The child had died a short time after
birth. Understandably heartbroken, she began to blame
her mother-in-law for all of her problems. Evidently, the
anger Nancy had held inside eventually manifested as a
uterine tumor.

She was advised to break through her resentment and
to find ways in which her feelings could be expressed
more constructively. From the reports on file, it appears

that she was able to follow the advice. As a result of the physical suggestions, her blood condition improved, and surgery could be performed. However, rather than having surgery, Nancy became convinced that she could eradicate the tumor herself (through absorption) by simply maintaining the Cayce recommendations and focusing upon her complete change in attitude. Thankfully, her chosen course of treatment worked. In 1941, she wrote that rather than being worried about the tumor, "My chief concern now is how I can best be of service with the understanding that is mine each day." (264-31 Reports) Later reports state that Nancy was able to transform herself. She wrote that she had been able to replace her resentment with an attitude of love and service. In 1956, at the age of sixty-six, she reported that she was "alive and well today as a result of having followed those readings." Twelve years later, in her late seventies she was still vitally interested in the work of A.R.E.

A thirty-one-year-old woman who was angry with her own mother and frustrated about her life events was advised that a change in attitude could best be had by being of service to someone else:

> Administering to others is the best way to help self. More individuals become so anxious about their own troubles, and yet helping others is the best way to rid yourself of your own troubles . . . Then what are you grumbling about because you dislike your mother? She dislikes you as much, but change this into love. Be kind, be gentle, be patient, be longsuffering, for if thy God was not longsuffering with thee, what chance would you have? 5081-1

In another case, a thirty-eight-year-old high school math teacher was told that, through the use of her will, she would determine whether she became in life "either

very, *very* good or at times *awful!*" (2487-1) In one of her
most recent incarnations, she had served as a private
tutor, teaching wealthy children subjects such as music,
painting, home economics, embroidering, dressmaking,
poetry, and English. In spite of a variety of personal hardships in that incarnation, she had gained for her service
to others. However, in an earlier incarnation in Greece,
she had been an associate of an individual in a position
of power and authority and had sometimes misused her
influence because of her own hatred and jealousy. For
that she had lost. Because both of these experiences bore
a heavy influence upon her present, the course of her
life would be determined by how she chose to exercise
her birthright of free will, especially as it related to her
relationships with other people.

The importance of individuals choosing to exercise
their wills, rather than allowing another person to dominate their lives, is illustrated in the case of Evelyn
Zimmerman, who acquired a reading in 1936. Evelyn
came seeking guidance on her life's direction, especially
in relation to her husband, with whom she was having
difficulties. In spite of the fact that she had been in-
stantly attracted to him when they first met, telling her
sister, "I've met the man I'm going to marry," she was
quickly disillusioned after their marriage. Her husband
drank heavily and gambled away what salary he earned.
For fifteen years, she tried everything she could to help
him, but to no avail. She didn't feel that she was strong
enough to leave him, and she was very confused about
her proper course of action. Only when she had become
physically sick from worry and having nowhere else to
turn did she seek out help in the form of a reading.

Cayce told Evelyn that her present challenges had the
potential to be a purposeful experience. The reading
traced the cause of the situation to an earlier incarnation in Greece. In that lifetime, a great spiritual teacher

had provided Evelyn with a philosophy and an approach to life that was truly transformational. She learned much and made great strides in her own personal development. Unfortunately, she later rejected those very truths because of the influence of the same man who was now her husband. She had lost spiritually because of her inability to exercise her free will in the right direction. In this life, her challenge was to choose to do what she knew to be right. In counseling her regarding the situation, her reading stated:

> Not of self-choosing an easier way; not of self attempting to escape that as is necessary for thine own understanding, thine own soul development; but rather ever, "Thy will, O Lord, be done in and through me—Use me as Thou seest I have need of, that I may be a *living* example of thy love, of thy guidance in this material experience." 845-4

Later, when Evelyn asked whether or not she should separate from her husband, Cayce responded, "This must be a choice within self. Self's own development is in jeopardy. Choose thou." Evidently, Evelyn needed to realize that she had to leave her husband, not as an escape from a difficult experience, but rather because she had to consider how she was destroying herself by remaining in the situation.

Eventually, Evelyn was able to leave her husband and, in time, the two divorced. She became very interested in the spiritual information contained in the Cayce material, even joining a spiritual discussion group, and began to rediscover some of the same truths she had once rejected in ancient Greece. According to notes on file, friends remarked how her choices had enabled Evelyn to become a much happier person. She truly enjoyed spending her time in being of service to others. Finally, she had allowed herself to exercise her will in the most positive direction.

A contemporary example discussing the apparent dichotomy between God's will and an individual's will is told in the story of Yvonne Eloise. Now in her early forties, Yvonne states that her philosophy can be summed up in one sentence: "God knows what we need better than we know what we want!" That philosophy is at the foundation of her concept of how free will really works:

> Many people associate freedom with the use of their free will. They have a hard time accepting the concept of God's will. They often think that doing God's will means giving up their own will. In fact, we should use our will to do God's! It is only when we totally surrender to God and accept His will as ours that we are free indeed. This may sound paradoxical; however, freedom at the soul level does not mean being able to use our will, but to use it for finding and living the truth.

In attempting to discover God's will for her own life, Yvonne has adopted a quote from Paul Twitchell, founder of the Eckankar religion: "Never indulge in blame, shame, or regret." She is also convinced that using forgiveness is one of the truest means of discovering the Creator's will for each individual's life. Yvonne's approach to working on soul development has come to her, not as a quaint philosophy but as a result of some very challenging experiences.

At the age of four, Yvonne's family had to evacuate the French colony of Algeria when the country became independent. Her family was forced to leave behind everything except for five suitcases and approximately five hundred dollars. There was no government assistance for those who evacuated, and Yvonne's childhood was filled with stories of her parents' struggle to raise two small children. The family spent a cold winter inside a stable. Much of their food consisted of wild vegetables: dandelions, leeks, asparagus, and mushrooms. In spite of their difficulties, they helped other refugees who were even worse off than they were themselves. The experience caused Yvonne to mature rapidly and to feel different from other children her own age. The family survived and made a life for themselves in France.

A second great challenge occurred when Yvonne was eighteen. She was involved in a serious car accident and nearly died. Her brother was driving, going much too fast on a rainy, slippery road. The car skidded during a turn, and Yvonne's brother lost control. The spin caused the car to hit a truck coming from the opposite direction. Her brother was thrown from the car and landed on his feet—miraculously, his only injury was a sprained ankle. Yvonne was not as lucky. The impact caused her to break the side window with her shoulder before being ejected from the car and landing in a muddy ditch.

Although Yvonne has no recollection of the scene, she broke her spine, her right shoulder blade, and her collarbone. Her lungs were so badly damaged that she had to be placed on a respirator immediately. The doctors at the hospital told her family that Yvonne was paralyzed and had no chance of survival. At first they were concerned about performing any emergency surgery because of the condition of her lungs, but eventually they went ahead, since there appeared to be nothing to lose. When she survived the operation, everyone said it was "a miracle." When she was released from the hospital three weeks later and sent to a rehabilitation center, it was another miracle. In time, she relearned how to walk, defying the doctor's pronouncement of paralysis.

Even during the painful challenge of teaching herself how to walk again, Yvonne felt compassion and empathy for those in rehabilitation who were worse off than she. She also learned patience and determination in striving to regain as much of her mobility as possible:

> I also learned to be grateful to God. Gratitude is an extremely important notion. It is healing; it brings joy and hope; it activates prayers; it strengthens relationships. Another thing I learned was that pity from others can be very destructive and depressing if expressed in a negative way. The vibrations people put out by thinking or saying, "Poor you," "This is terrible," etc., can make someone feel even more his or her own disability or problems. Being cheerful and treating the person as if he or she were perfectly all right is often much better. If we really want to help people who are going through difficulties of any kind—physically, mentally or spiritually—the best way is to look beyond the problem and invite God's presence. We may have compassion and feel terrible for someone, but expressing it in front of that person may not be of help. It only brings more negative energy to the situation, emphasizing the difficulties.

Today, Yvonne is a highly educated business professional and a respected part of an international corporation. She still feels some effects from her accident, including difficulty walking; however, she is not angry or upset about anything that has happened in her life. In fact, in spite of Yvonne's humbleness and unassuming nature, she is often pointed out as one of the most optimistic and inspiring individuals in the firm. In discussing her belief that love and forgiveness are instrumental ingredients for soul development, Yvonne has some concluding words regarding her life philosophy:

We continually meet self. Therefore, we are entirely responsible for whatever happens to us. We are *not* victims. We must stop blaming others. Others are merely instruments that the Universal Forces use to have us meet ourselves. Consequently, when something "bad" happens to us, it is always for a reason, and ultimately for our own good—if we try to learn the lesson behind it. When something bad occurs, it is because we are reaping what we sowed in the past, because we have a lesson to learn from that experience, or because we accepted the situation at the soul level as a mission.

As Yvonne's story demonstrates, the human will has a tremendous influence upon how we choose to experience life. Two individuals might encounter the very same situation and yet their experience of that situation will be dependent upon their attitudes, their perceptions, and the choices they eventually make. For that reason, ultimately, each of us can choose from at least three different responses to life and to any situation that crosses our path. In simplest terms, we can use our wills to respond to life as a *victim*, as a *bystander*, or as a *conscious cocreator*.

Although few individuals might believe, let alone verbalize, the fact that they have chosen to respond to life as a victim, this behavioral response has become extremely popular in contemporary society. The predominant attitude in victim consciousness is one in which an individual begins to believe that the condition of one's life is primarily dependent upon what other people have done or because of the experiences the person has encountered. Victim consciousness can occur whenever an individual desires to somehow escape from the things that life has presented. This same consciousness is responsible for blaming our parents, our upbringing, our neighbors, our society, our family, and even our karma for our present situation. The attitude of allowing one's self to be a victim is expressed whenever an individual holds such thoughts in mind as: "I am no longer responsible for the things that happen to me" and "The condition of my life is because of what other people have done to me." Victim consciousness is that part of us that shirks personal responsibility.

In today's society, many people seem to be overwhelmed by relationship problems, financial difficulties, job insecurities, family tragedies, and all manner of physical, mental, and spiritual hardship. It is not that these things are necessarily new to the human condition; instead, it appears as though many people are undergoing "changing times" of one kind or another at this same period in our collective history. Perhaps it is because of the preponderance of these personal challenges that victim consciousness has skyrocketed. According to the *Statistical Abstract of the United States*, the number of private lawsuits filed in this country rose from approximately 29,000 in 1960 to more than 270,000 thirty-five years later! In large part, this increase is due to the fact that many of us now disavow or refuse to accept personal responsibility in our life situations: "Someone did something to me, and therefore I need to sue them."

From the perspective of the Edgar Cayce readings, the truth of the matter is that each of us is very much involved in the creation of our life experiences as well as the attitude with which we choose to meet them. Our option is not whether we want to be involved or even responsible in the process; instead, it seems to be one in which we have the opportunity to be conscious or unconscious about our participation. A reading given to a forty-four-year-old woman put a humorous twist on this same idea when she asked, "Is there likelihood of bad health in March?" Cayce responded, "If you are looking for it you can have it in February! If you want to skip March, skip it—you'll have it in June! If you want to skip June, don't have it at all this year!" (3564-1)

In terms of someone having the opportunity to think like a victim but choosing not to, Paula Jenkins is an example. All of her life, her single strongest desire was to have children. She admits that her hardest lesson has been to live with the fact that she is growing older and is a single adult with no chance of having any children of her own—a series of lumpectomies and a hysterectomy have convinced her that motherhood is not her life's path. However, rather than seeing herself as a victim of circumstance, Paula has found fulfillment through service work, through her pursuit of an education that has enabled her to become an interpreter for the hearing-impaired, and through her desire to be involved with a hospice organization and terminally ill children.

Allowing oneself to respond to life as a victim can occur even in the simplest of interactions with other people. The readings told one fifty-three-year-old man that his greatest fault was that he was too sensitive to criticism and took it personally whenever someone was simply joking with him. That tendency had created a dynamic in which he often saw himself as the brunt of jokes and the object of faultfinding, and he responded to people and events as a victim. As a result, he had caused himself to undergo "many a hardship in the present experience." (1876-1) He was advised to quit taking everything personally, "when such is not always meant," and, instead, to use his talent for sensitivity in aiding other people.

On another occasion, Cayce told a thirty-four-year-old man with multiple sclerosis that one of the first steps in his healing process needed to be a change in his attitude. It was suggested that the man consider using the following: "'The physical conditions that have come upon me are those most necessary for my own soul's development.'" (716-2)

In another example, a thirty-six-year-old professor of chemical engineering was counseled that, regardless of his present situation or difficulties, there is always the possibility of responding to life in a positive manner:

> . . . ye can do something about it! For know that ye are in the present experience, in the present environ, in the present years of thy activity more productive, more far-reaching in the influence ye have, in the opportunity that ye will have for making the earth a better place to live in for those to come. And remember you'll be back again! What do you want it to look like? . . . you'd better be up and doing . . . 4047-2

Regardless of how things may appear in life, the perspective of the Edgar Cayce readings is that we are not victims. Life is a purposeful experience if we only choose to make it so. Because of our relationship with the Creator, there is always the possibility of hope and change.

A second approach to life, no more positive than victim consciousness, is when an individual responds to life's events as a *bystander*. This is when we become upset or depressed by a situation or a problem "out there," but don't take any measures to address the issue personally. This is when people get excited about positive changes in the world but don't necessarily see any need to make positive changes in their own lives. This is when we imagine that one of these days—"When I have more money," or "When I have more time," or "When I feel a little better"—"I'm going to get serious about doing the things that I know I should do."

A fascinating case from the Cayce files presented itself in 1934, demonstrating how a soul can actually choose to do nothing with his or her life in any given sojourn. A twenty-six-year-old man named Gary received a life reading and was told that his soul history provided a beautiful illustration of the power of the human will. Gary learned that, in a past incarnation, he had been the brother of Solomon, Hebrew king and builder of the Great Temple. In spite of the fact that they had been related, apparently each brother exercised the power of his will in very different directions. Solomon used opportunities, while his brother did not. During the course of the reading, Cayce stated:

> For, while the entity was an associate or a brother of Solomon in an experience, what one did with his knowledge and understanding and what the other did with his understanding made for quite a difference in each one's position in that experience and the sojourns of each soul in other experiences. 476-1

Gary's past incarnations included a lifetime when he persecuted individuals for their susceptibility to visions, dreams, and various psychic experiences. Because of the influence of that lifetime, he was drawn to the subject matter but confused by the meaning of such experiences. Previously, in a French sojourn, Gary had been a military leader of some prominence. Unfortunately, he used his talent for destruction, satisfying personal grudges, rather than for mobilizing his people toward a greater cause. His lifetime in Palestine during the reign of Solomon had included a great many advantages; however, they had not been used, especially for things of a spiritual nature. Although Gary had undoubtedly received many of the same opportunities as Solomon, his choices and the use of his will had negated many of his spiritual opportunities. Apparently, he had not chosen to do anything with the spiritual information that had been at his disposal. The reading advised him not to make the same choice again:

> For, the spiritual life should direct and the social, the moral, the material things should be rather the outgrowth for every soul . . . Be willing to be used as the channel of the blessing, *a* blessing, *many* blessings, to others . . .

In contemporary society, an example of a bystander would be an individual who anxiously anticipates a new world of peace, harmony, and love and yet makes no effort to bring those same ingredients into the world in everyday life. From Cayce's perspective, until individuals throughout the world begin to work with and build the ingredients of a new world into their present experience, we are never going to be able to get there.

Another way of looking at this idea is to realize that the road upon which we're traveling has got to include elements of where we wish to head or else the road and the goal will never meet. Those individuals who are anxiously anticipating a new world order of peace, harmony, love, understanding, and community with the entire world but are not doing anything to bring those very qualities into their present experience are only fooling themselves.

From Cayce's perspective, it is also impossible to be idle and not have an impact upon the world around us. The truth of the matter is that we are always cocreating, either in attunement or out of alignment with the Whole. If this is true, if we are always building for the future, what are individuals creating by their fascination with earthquakes, with their need to buy guns, with their bigotry and hatred, and with their personal arguments and animosities? Cayce told one individual, "Know that thoughts are things, and as their currents run they may become crimes or miracles." (2419-1) With this in mind, we need to become cognizant of whether our thoughts are creating miracles for the future or contributing to possible disaster. For that reason, the readings suggest that the best approach to life is to use the human will as a *conscious cocreator.*

Because of our relationship with God, we are always in the process of cocreating our lives. However, that cocreative capacity can be unconscious and negative, or it can be conscious and positive. An example from the readings is the case of a forty-two-year-old male opera singer who was experiencing health problems and was warned that he needed to exercise his will in a positive direction or else he would draw to himself very negative consequences. One of his most prominent incarnations from the past had been as a high priest who had "gained and lost, gained and lost" in terms of his own soul development. He had gained for his efforts in bringing hope to those who had lost their way. He had lost, however, when his popularity led to many opportunities for self-glorification and self-indulgence. From that experience, he maintained an innate desire to seek out personal gratification and pleasure. He was advised that his life direction and his health were deeply connected to the choices he made. Cayce counseled him with a warning:

> Beware that a worse fate does not befall thee in the present, then, by making applications of self in that as will become a hopeful experience in the lives of those who are dependent upon the entity not only for the material things but for the ability of the entity to create hope within the mental self—which is in every entity and in every soul . . . 1437-1

Conscious cocreators are individuals who realize their

responsibility in shaping the course of their lives. A conscious cocreator understands that each of us is responsible for the present *now* that was once our collective future. Rather than approaching life as a victim, a conscious cocreator faces life's experiences as opportunities to respond in the best possible manner. A conscious cocreator sees life's lessons as integral components of soul growth and personal development.

To be sure, most often individuals respond to life in a variety of ways, sometimes choosing to be a victim, on occasion acting as a bystander, and in other situations choosing to be conscious in terms of what they are creating. However, it is only when we decide to take responsibility for our lives and become a conscious cocreator that we have any hope of creating personal and lasting change, helping ourselves and others in the process.

In contemporary society, our choosing to become a conscious cocreator suggests that we can no longer think that God (or someone else) is going to bring about an age of peace and enlightenment and all we have to do is wait for it. The time has come to become cognizant of our personal responsibility in creating a brand new world and a paradigm shift in our collective understanding regarding what life is really about. In fact, unless we begin to respond to life in this manner, we are actually making global problems and personal difficulties worse. Cayce reminded a thirty-four-year-old woman, "For ye are as a corpuscle in the body of God; thus a co-creator with Him, in what ye think, in what ye do. And ye change each soul ye contact . . . no soul may come in contact with the entity without being changed, either in body, in mind or in purpose." (2794-3)

In the Cayce cosmology, neither one's personal nor collective future is fixed. Instead, both are inextricably linked to what each of us decides to do with the human will and the choices life presents to us. Although it is true that our destiny is to realize and, eventually, manifest our deep connection to the Creator, the timing of that realization is entirely up to each individual. Only to the extent that we are able to set aside our personality self and express our individuality self will we realize that, ultimately, what we really want is exactly what God has wanted for us all along. In time, we will come to the inevitable conclusion that free will is not primarily about doing what we want but about becoming who we really are.

What if we realized that our perceptions and our choices truly create the life we experience? What if we understood that, regardless of what occurs in our lives, it can become a positive experience if only we choose to make it so? What if we decided to become conscious of what we are creating for ourselves and the world around us? What if we suddenly became aware of the fact that our future is not dependent upon *what* we know, but on *how well* we apply whatever we know?

Keys to Spiritual Growth:
Ideals, Attunement, and
Application

Then, as to whether there are developments or retardments through this particular sojourn will depend upon what the entity holds as its ideal, *and what it does in its mental and material relationships* respecting *that ideal!*   2444-1

(Q) Any other advice that will be of help for this entity at this time?
(A) Keep the face toward the light and the shadows will fall behind.   310-3

What if the Creator were actively involved in our transformational process? What if much more than wanting us to succeed, God actually destines that each soul *will* succeed, that it is simply a matter of time? What if one's spiritual growth were not dependent upon religion but were available to everyone regardless of creed? What if

134

soul development actually consists of three simple steps: setting spiritual ideals, working with personal attunement, and then applying what one knows to do? What if everyone makes it eventually?

In the Cayce cosmology, one of the most important steps in soul growth is setting spiritual ideals. This process enables individuals to create a "guide map" for personal spiritual growth. A guide map includes not only a person's spiritual aspirations but also the mental attitudes and the physical activities that can help facilitate and nurture the ideal with which an individual has chosen to work. Without such a guide, the mundane things of life can too easily take precedence and fill the day's events. In other words, we make time to watch our favorite television show or finish a project that seems important to us, but how often do we give the same level of priority to spiritual growth, meditation, service, prayer— all the things that we might consider important to soul development? A guide map of spiritual ideals and the corresponding attitudes and activities to make them real can be extremely helpful in this regard.

A story emphasizing how the things of the spirit should have a prominent place in life is provided by the case history of Samuel, who received a life reading in 1931. Referred by friends, Samuel was a thirty-eight-year-old furniture manufacturer with great hopes for the future. To some, he was a dreamer and a visionary. One of his greatest desires was the establishment of a major motion picture studio in Virginia Beach, Virginia.

In detailing his soul's history, Cayce told Samuel that his previous incarnations included a number of former lifetimes when he had learned to be of service to others. Most recently, he had gained for his service to settlers during the establishment of the Georgia colony under the direction of Governor James Oglethorpe. Unfortunately, Samuel had also lost in that sojourn for his seeking of vengeance when he became disillusioned with the governor for promises that had not been kept. Another gain for service rendered had been acquired in the Germanic lands at the time of the Roman period. Being quick to assist those in need, Samuel was praised for having operated with a motto that seemed to keep in mind: " . . . as is sown, so shall the harvest be . . . " In that same incarnation, he had eventually come to the conclusion that service done to assist another individual was its own reward.

In spite of his innate desire to be of service, however, and because of other past-life influences, Samuel was warned not to fall into a pattern of dwelling upon whatever divisions and divisiveness existed among people. He was encouraged to begin seeing beyond the different ideas people have about things and to find, instead, what they have in common—an ideal upon which they all can agree. If he responded in this manner, Samuel was assured that he possessed a deep love for people that would enable him to put them first.

He also was counseled to let his focus on things of a spiritual nature take precedence over his desire for a motion picture studio:

> In *this* may the entity find the greater development in the present. Make for self those that make the spiritual or soul development, and the answer from *material* forces *for* physical desires will be the natural *result*, and not *make* physical desires the aim or purpose. 2122-1

Hundreds of people received this same advice regarding the importance of placing an emphasis on spiritual ideals. One of those was a forty-seven-year-old engineer who was instructed: "First, know thy ideal—spiritually, mentally, materially. Not so much as to what you would

like others to be, but what may be *your* ideal relationships to others!" (1998-1) He was encouraged to use his
creativity and his energies to discover how he could begin serving the purpose of the whole rather than himself
or any individual part.

This focus on the individual evaluating self and then
becoming an example of what she or he would like to
see in others was expressed to a thirty-eight-year-old
naval officer when Cayce asked him to consider: "What
sort of a church would that church be if every member
was just like yourself? What would it look like? What sort
of home life would there be, if every husband was just
like yourself? What is the ideal attitude of a husband, of a
father? What is the ideal attitude of a neighbor? of a
rancher? of a brother?" (5400-1)

Similar advice was given to a thirty-three-year-old
Jewish housewife who obtained a reading and asked how
she might better demonstrate spiritual truths to others.
Cayce advised her that the best approach would be
through her own example. She was encouraged to eradicate all thoughts and patterns from within herself that
were out of keeping with her awareness of what wholeness and soul development would suggest for her personally. As to how to make this practical in her daily life,
the reading suggested that she focus upon ideals that
would help bolster the fruits of the spirit. Suggestions
given to her were to put into practice such things as compassion, hope, brotherly love, faith, and fellowship. She
was encouraged to cultivate these ideals also within herself, for whatever the mind focuses upon becomes a
larger part of who one is as an individual:

> . . . as the body thinks, as the body limits itself in
> any *negative* influence, then it becomes aware in
> that direction. As the body embraces all as a posi-
> tive influence or force, more and more does the

growth come to the awareness of *making* itself, the soul, at-one with the Creative Forces. See? 903-23

The importance of establishing spiritual ideals was explained to people of all ages and from all walks of life. From Cayce's perspective, this process is inextricably connected to whether or not a soul ultimately succeeds or fails in any given incarnation.

A twenty-three-year-old designer who obtained a life reading was interested in finding out, in part, whether or not her fiancé was the man she was supposed to marry. She was informed that, ultimately, the answer depended upon what ideals each was working with in their respective lives. If they worked with spiritual ideals and aspirations that were complementary, then they could build a relationship in which "they may be one." However, if their ideals were not in keeping with one another, then Cayce warned the woman that a marriage relationship between her and her fiancé "would not be well." (451-2)

Parents of an eleven-year-old girl seeking advice for their daughter's growth and development were informed that the various incarnations, patterns, and desires within an individual are often at war because they can be very different from one another. This inner struggle frequently results in all kinds of personal problems and confusion. The parents were advised that one of the best ways they could assist their daughter was to help her in establishing a spiritual ideal. Afterward, they needed to encourage her to align her daily activities with the mental attitudes and aspirations that would best reflect that ideal. In this manner, the various patterns within her would no longer be vying for her attention (405-1).

The importance of overcoming negative patterns and selfish desires in order to achieve soul development was also pointed out to a forty-two-year-old naturopathic physician. Cayce said that because these patterns had never been adequately addressed in the soul's history, a number of life experiences had been wasted, resulting in soul regression.

The physician's past lives included an incarnation as one of Leonardo DaVinci's assistants. Although he had received much soul prompting from higher levels at the time because of the wondrous things with which DaVinci was involved, he had failed to use them as a guiding principle in his life. According to the reading, rather than being able to see the spiritual import of much of their work, "the entity wasted much of its ability in riotous living . . . " (490-1)

In another life in Atlantis as a physician and scientist, he had experimented with the curative properties of derivatives from minerals, plants, and animals. Although his scientific work had proven helpful, the reading suggested that his personal development had not been at the same level and beyond reproach. In fact, he had spent much time in a focused pursuit of purely carnal pleasures. Because these tendencies (and others) remained a part of his soul, he was advised to work with his ideals and to set a higher intention. Apparently, his soul development was at a standstill until he learned to put himself aside and focus his energies into being of service to others.

A forty-three-year-old housewife who had once worked as a milliner was told that her recurring dream of a row of black houses along the Chicago River was a valid memory from her most recent life near Fort Dearborn. In an earlier sojourn in France, she had been one who specialized in bodily adornments and hats. But the life that had served her the most had been in Arabia, when she had found and applied a spiritual ideal. Although the reading suggested that she had lost her desire to apply spiritual principles during the latter portion of that Arabian incarnation when she had been an old woman, for the most part she had succeeded: " . . . not *only* did the entity give *self* in attempting to make this ideal applicable in the entity's *experience,* but desirous of—and did give—much of the teachings to her own people . . . " (340-15)

In the present, she was encouraged to again find her personal relationship with the Creator and to begin applying those things that would better enable her to bring joy, peace, understanding, and service into her relationships with others. Cayce promised her that as she was faithful to whatever it was she knew to do, even more light and more understanding would find their way into her life.

The readings' approach to creating a guide map or ideals chart with which to begin a plan for personal soul development is really quite simple. Repeatedly, Cayce advised that all we need to do is to take a piece of paper and draw three columns. The first column should be labeled *My Spiritual Ideal;* the second, *My Mental Attitudes;* and the third, *My Physical Activities.*

In the spiritual ideal column, Cayce told people to write a word or a phrase that best expressed the spiritual aspiration that she or he hoped to cultivate or emulate at that time. Examples include such things as compassion, love, or understanding. The readings also suggested that some people might wish to write down the name of a spiritual leader who best embodied the example they wished to imitate, such as Jesus, Buddha, Abraham, or Mohammed. However, people were often encouraged to select a spiritual ideal that they would really begin to work with in their lives. If someone needed to be more patient or more understanding in interactions with others, then that might be an appropriate spiritual ideal with which to begin working.

Selecting a spiritual ideal is not a one-time process;

the ideal changes over time as the need to select something new or more challenging arises. With this in mind, Cayce asked a forty-six-year-old woman, "What is the ideal relationship which should exist between self, home, friends, activities in relation to things as well as conditions, as well as experiences? Change these as there is unfoldment in the study of thine own self." (3051-6)

For ease of explanation, let's imagine that you select compassion as the spiritual ideal to cultivate. With this in mind, you would write *compassion* under the spiritual ideal column. Under the second column, you would list all of those attitudes that could promote the aspiration of compassion in every area in life. Perhaps you would decide that such attitudes as forgiveness, love, understanding, openness, and even compassion itself would be appropriate mental attitudes. You should choose at least five to seven attitudes (or more) that could help create and build an opportunity for the spiritual ideal to be expressed in the mental realm.

It is important that the mental attitudes provide you with a broad enough scope to be applicable in every area of your life. For example, perhaps openness might best describe the mental attitude you want to work with in a challenging work relationship. Maybe forgiveness is the approach you choose with regard to a child. Possibly patience best describes the attitude you choose in relationship to self. The ideals chart should take into account every area of your life.

The third column is the most detailed. It is where you list all of the physical *activities* that will help to manifest the mental attitudes reflecting the spiritual ideal. For every attitude, there should be at least two or three corresponding activities that you can begin doing in your relationship with other individuals. For example, with the spiritual ideal of compassion, a corresponding attitude might be love. In this case, the activities column should detail actions you plan to carry out in order to better express love toward others as well as toward self. In terms of writing out an activity directed toward others that could manifest an attitude of love, perhaps you would write, "to verbally express feelings of love every day." Another activity could be "to do something loving toward another person without thought of receiving anything in return." An activity that might enable you to express love toward self might be to "stop saying (or even thinking) 'I can't,'" or "to make a list of loving affirmations that are put up around the house" to be read to yourself, such as "You are a child of God, and therefore a channel of His love."

From Cayce's perspective, an ideals chart or guide map simply creates a step-by-step approach for bringing spiritual ideals into the material world. As we apply spiritual principles in everyday life, they become a part of personal awareness, and soul development is the result. To be sure, as you work with ideals, you'll discover that your ideals might need to become more challenging with the passage of time.

Although the readings encouraged people to choose a personal ideal, they also asserted that, ultimately, these ideals all lead to the same goal. One person was told, "There is *one* way, but there are many paths." (3083-1) All souls are heading toward the same spiritual goal in their ongoing process of soul development. Whether we want to label that goal *perfection* or *Christ Consciousness* or *God Consciousness* or *Buddha Consciousness* or whatever term with which we feel comfortable, the end result is the same. Therefore, our smaller ideals (such as aspects of love, service, kindness) simply serve as incremental steps toward personal soul development.

In the Cayce cosmology, the ultimate purpose of life is to bring an awareness of spirit into the earth, assisting in the transformation of oneself and others in the process.

For that reason, just as important as the establishment of spiritual ideals to act as a directional beacon in one's life is the activity of *personal attunement.* As we work with ideals and then attune to the Divine within, we become more aware of our spiritual nature, our connection to one another, and our relationship with the Creator. Simply stated, attunement is the process through which we reawaken to our true self, our individuality, and our spiritual nature. The most frequently recommended tools for achieving this attunement are the regular practices of prayer and meditation.

Beginning in 1931, Edgar Cayce gave a series of readings to an ecumenical prayer group studying meditation, prayer, and spiritual healing. Cayce saw both prayer and meditation as communication vehicles for getting in touch with the Divine. In one instance, he told the group:

What *is* Meditation? It is not musing, not daydreaming; but as ye find your bodies made up of the physical, mental and spiritual, it is the attuning of the mental body and the physical body to its spiritual source. 281-41

The readings suggested that prayer is essentially talking to God, whereas meditation is quieting the personality self and training the individual to attune to the relationship with the Creator: "For prayer is supplication for direction, for understanding. Meditation is listening to the Divine within." (1861-19) Cayce also said that meditation is something that each person needs to learn, just as we learned to walk or to talk. He once told a twenty-eight-year-old man that he had spent enough time studying and reading about spiritual principles and that it was now time to learn how to meditate (436-3).

When a forty-nine-year-old accountant asked how he

could be of the greatest service to humankind, Cayce
recommended that he begin working with the daily
practice of prayer and meditation. In this manner, God
could use him as a channel of love and service to others.
It was promised that in the process, he would also discover a greater sense of peace, happiness, and joy in his
own life. In suggesting a practical approach for working
with meditation, the reading advised:

> . . . setting aside a definite time, a period during
> each day's activity when there will be the purifying
> of the body, as in accord with that which would
> make for consecrating of self in all of its efforts, all
> of its abilities, and entering into the holy of holies
> within self for that talk with thy God within thyself.
> 270-33

Although some approaches to meditation suggest that
the mind gets in the way of the meditator and must
therefore be blanked out, the readings assert that whatever the mind dwells upon—whether in meditation or
by constant thought—becomes a greater portion of the
individual. For that reason, the mind can be a powerful
tool for attunement as well as for personal soul development. In order to assist people in directing their mental
processes in more positive directions, Cayce often provided spiritual "affirmations" that could be used for
meditation or personal contemplation. (Note: See the
end of this chapter for a selection of such affirmations.)
Using the readings' approach, anyone can have a period of meditation by following a few simple steps. First,
get into a comfortable position. It is probably best to sit
in a chair, keeping your spine straight, your feet flat on
the floor, and your eyes closed. Find a comfortable place
for your hands, either in your lap or at your sides. In order to help with a balanced flow of energy throughout

the physical body, the readings suggest keeping your palms face down against your legs or closed against your stomach. Slowly take a few deep breaths and begin to relax. Breathe the air deep into your lungs, hold it for a moment, and then slowly breathe it out. With your mind, search your body for any obvious tension or tight muscles. You can try to relieve the tension by deep breathing, by imagining the area relaxing, or by gently massaging any tightness with your fingertips. When you have become comfortable and more at ease, you are ready to move on.

Take another deep, relaxing breath and begin to focus your mind on a single, peaceful, calming thought. Instead of thinking about what went on at work or what has to be accomplished with the remainder of your day, try focusing on a spiritual affirmation or even a single thought such as "I am at peace" or a spiritual phrase such as "The love of God fills my being." These thoughts or affirmations become the focal point for your meditation period.

The first stage of meditation involves thinking about the message of your affirmation. In one of the above examples, you would think about the words, "I am at peace." After a few moments of thinking the words, you should be able to move onto the second stage of meditation, which is feeling the meaning behind those words. For example, you could continue saying, "I am at peace"; however, the feeling behind these words can be much more meaningful than the actual words themselves. As an example of how a *feeling* is more all encompassing than a thought, consider saying the words, "I love my child," vs. the feeling behind those words. From Cayce's perspective, whenever individuals are able to hold the feeling of the affirmation throughout their entire being, they are truly meditating and building the focus of the affirmation within themselves.

During this second stage of meditation, try to hold the feeling of the affirmation in silent attention without needing to repeat the words. Whenever the mind begins to wander, simply bring your focus back to the words of the affirmation. Once again, you would begin by thinking the words of the affirmation and then by trying to concentrate on the feeling behind those words. Don't become discouraged if you find yourself thinking more about distractions than focusing upon the affirmation— it takes practice. To begin with, you might want to spend anywhere from three to fifteen minutes trying to hold the affirmation silently. Longer meditation periods will become possible with practice and experience.

To close a meditation period, the readings emphasize the importance of consciously sending out prayers and good thoughts to other people and situations in life. At this point, you may wish to open the palms to enable the energy of meditation to flow through them. Since we do not always know what may be best for another's personal growth and development, it is recommended that you simply pray that the individual be surrounded by light, love, and God's will, presence, and protection rather than praying for something specific. As you begin to practice meditation daily, it will become easier. You might also discover that the feeling you have been focusing upon in meditation will actually begin to carry over into greater portions of the day.

Perhaps more than anything else, attunement is essential for coming to a true understanding of who and what we really are. As stated previously, in Cayce's worldview, the end result of soul development is that all individuals will eventually realize their true spiritual self and their connection to the Whole.

The readings told a thirty-six-year-old attorney that this realization was actually the ultimate cause of each soul's creation in the first place:

What then is the purpose of the entity's activity in the consciousness of mind, matter, spirit in the present?

That it, the entity, may *know* itself to *be* itself and part of the Whole; not the Whole but one *with* the whole; and thus retaining its individuality, knowing itself to be itself yet one with the purposes of the First Cause that called it, the entity, into *being*, into the awareness, into the consciousness of itself. 826-11

Cayce went on to say that, because the soul has an "affinity" to things of a spiritual nature, it is simply natural law that enables each individual to attune to divine will. Through the regular practice of meditation, the attorney was promised that he would become aware of his companionship with God, as well as what he needed to do in order to apply spiritual principles in his everyday interactions with others. The reading encouraged him to set ideals, to begin to meditate, and then to apply whatever it was he knew to do: "In *applying* that ye know *today!* and tomorrow the next step is given. For it is line upon line, precept upon precept, here a little, there a little."

Another individual was encouraged to work with some of the same methods of attunement that he had used in previous incarnations. During an earlier lifetime in Tibet, he had apparently relied upon the inspiration and mysteries of the Vedas. A sojourn in Ethiopia had enabled him to come in contact with one of Jesus' disciples, giving him the opportunity to become grounded in spiritual truths. At that same time, he had become adept at using chanting, affirmations, and meditation to awaken to a state of inner attunement. He was advised to use these same tools in the present (315-4).

In addition to the discovery of an awareness of the Divine through meditation and prayer, the readings make it clear that, because of the nature of humankind—

spiritual beings undergoing the limitations of physical consciousness—we can also experience personal attunement in a variety of ways. Examples include suddenly having an instant awareness of the presence of the Divine, finding oneself in an expanded level of consciousness, or, perhaps, encountering extraordinary dreams.

Olive Karnes, for example, discusses a number of instances in which she has somehow attuned to higher levels of awareness. Some of these experiences were foreign to her conservative Christian upbringing. One of the first occasions occurred when she met her husband and saw him wearing different clothes than those he actually wore. She had the overwhelming sense that she had known him before. Now, she looks back on that experience as a past-life memory—something that would have been inconceivable to her at the time. Other situations in which her consciousness seemed to expand happened after she began having marital problems:

I had a waking vision one night of Christ and the Virgin Mary. They said nothing, but I understood that, no matter what my difficulty, I would have the strength to face any trial, and they would be with me. After this experience, there were other dreams or visions that would show me or tell me of things to come in a storylike fashion. As I grew in the acceptance and understanding of these dreams, there were greater obstacles to face.

Several years later, I gave birth to a child who had a congenital heart defect. She was only here a short time, but the Lord spoke to me before her death, simply saying, "I want her back." After going through everything in my mind, I said, "Thy will be done." Within two weeks, she passed away (her doctors did not believe she would die).

The Lord spoke to me once more, five years later,

to warn me of my divorce ... My husband and I were at a picnic given by a friend, and my husband was sitting next to a woman whom we had just met that day, when I heard the words, "He is going to marry her." My first thought was, "He can't; he's married to me." A year later they were married.

Since that time, whenever there has been an important change in my life, I have experienced dreams ...

Harriet Jenkins tells the story of how an awareness of God's presence filled her mind when she was depressed over the unexpected death of her beloved cat. Because the veterinarian believed that the cat had died from an aggressive and contagious disease, Harriet was forced to bring her other two cats into the vet's office for evaluation and testing. She was depressed, extremely upset, and anxious about the visit. In her own words:

I dreaded this trip because my cats hate to be put into a carrier and driven anywhere, and I also feared I would lose them to the disease. Before leaving, I sat down on my bedroom floor and said a prayer to God, asking Him to take over and that I was putting this into His hands. I meditated for about five minutes (which I was not in the habit of doing) and a small voice said to me, "You love your cats more than you love Me." Then an amazing thing happened: My two cats went into their carriers like they knew it was where they needed to be. A calmness came to me then, and I realized that God was really listening to me and was going to help me through this. This was the first time in my life I had ever experienced such certainty that I was not alone.

When I arrived at the veterinarian's office, the anger again reared its ugly head. I felt the staff were not empathetic enough and were hardened to the suffering I was going through. As I waited in the treatment room, I again said a prayer asking that my anger be taken from my heart. I then heard a voice on the other side of the door, from a staff member saying, "I wish people would understand the long hours we put in and that we really do care." All of a sudden, the anger lifted from me and I felt such peace and an understanding of what the staff must be feeling and how hard it must be for them to have to go through this with me. When the anger dissolved, the sympathy the doctor and staff felt for my loss was then visible, and I was able to begin the healing process.

Harriet says that the experience taught her about God's ever-abiding presence and that all she needed to do was to open to an awareness of His presence "and listen." From that day forward, she felt confident that she would be provided with all the direction and guidance she needed for any situation, simply by asking for it.

Now in her seventies, Karen Lowell has had a lifetime of experiences that she believes have been invaluable in helping her grow and develop at a soul level. Through her roles as a wife, mother, and nurse, she has learned how to accept others, how to forgive, and how to love. She has also come to believe that "We are all following our own path—fulfilling the contract we made before this earthly incarnation. We all have lessons to be learned, each in our own way and, if not learned, we will come back over and over until we do."

One of the things that has been helpful to her is the realization that "Messages come from dreams," as a way of bringing information, enlightenment, and an awareness to the dreamer that transcends the limitations of ordinary consciousness. These dreams can often assist us in helping others or ourselves. One of the earliest dreams she remembers is of a friend named Hank who was in the air force during World War II:

> My dream was of an airplane landing in the river below my bedroom window. (We lived on an island in the St. Lawrence River.) Hank got out of the plane and waded through the water to the house. We were all so glad to see him—he was so handsome in his uniform, it's no wonder I had a schoolgirl crush on him.

Shortly after having the dream, Karen learned that Hank's plane had been shot down near Italy. As it turned out, he ended up floating on a raft for several days before being found. Her dream had given her an awareness of the situation and the fact that he would be okay, even before she learned about his predicament. From that time on, Karen was convinced that dreams can be extremely helpful in bringing information to people if they simply begin to work with them.

From the perspective of the Edgar Cayce information, soul growth is ultimately achieved through the consistent application of spiritual principles. With this in mind, a fifty-year-old woman who inquired about the best possible approach to soul development was told that the answer was simply personal attunement, followed by application. She was encouraged to attune to the highest Source she had within herself and then to pour out that spiritual energy in prayer, in her activities, and in her interactions with others (3357-2).

Other people were encouraged to include a balanced approach to application that would take into account the physical, the mental, and the spiritual aspects of themselves. Invariably, a balanced approach addresses physical health, well-being, exercise, and diet. Such an approach considers the importance of the mental things that the mind is focusing on: thoughts, literature, movies, etc. Finally, things of a spiritual nature such as prayer and meditation are also to be included. Cayce called this important balance a well-rounded approach. Specific advice along these lines was given to several people:

Then, be a well-*rounded* body. Take specific, *definite* exercises morning and evening. Make the body *physically*, as well as mentally, tired and those things that have been producing those conditions where sleep, inertia, poisons in system from non-eliminations, will disappear...

... for each cell of the blood stream, each corpuscle, is whole *universe* in itself. Do not eat like a canary and expect to do *manual* labor. Do not eat like a rail splitter and expect to do the work of a mind reader or a university professor...

So, in conducting thine own life—make the physical corrections necessary, yes—but make also thy mind and thine body, thine going in and thine coming out, thine activities day by day, consistent *with*—and the reward will be—an exemplary life, a *goodly* body, an *open* mind, a *loving* spirit! 341-31

Budget thy time more; first in the care for the physical being, recreation, improvement mentally, spiritually, also socially. Take time to be holy. Be holy purposefully, and ye will find much of that ye have looked for, hoped for, will come to thee in new environs, new surroundings.

... Thy ability to smile when everything has gone dead wrong, thy ability to see the ridiculous at times has saved the day for others as well as for self. 3393-2

For, the warnings have been given again and

again as to how to keep the body fit—as to the foods, the diets, the exercise, the recreation, the rest, the building of the mental body, the time to play and the time to work, the time to recuperate the mental body, the time to make holy and the time to pray.

All of these must be observed, if there would be a well-rounded, a well-centered life. 257-228

Don't let a day go by without meditation and prayer for some definite purpose, and not for self, but that self may be the channel of help to someone else. For in helping others is the greater way to help self.

Do take plenty of time for rest . . . take time to work, to think, to make contacts for a social life and for recreation. This old adage might well apply: After breakfast, work a while, after lunch rest a while, after dinner walk a mile. This as a recreation may be a helpful, balanced experience for this life. 3624-1

In addition to striving for a balanced life, a twenty-year-old man, who obtained a physical reading for a problem with his spine and his inability to concentrate, was advised to spend a part of each evening reflecting upon his day's events. Cayce recommended that he take the time to briefly note his experiences, thoughts, and activities for the entire day. Each night, he was to set this paper aside and then, the next day, continue working with ideals, attunement, and application, enabling the fruits of the Spirit to become a greater portion of his life. The following evening, he was to make the same type of journal of his day's events and the thoughts that had been on his mind. He was to follow this routine for a month. At the end of thirty days, he could look at his notations from the first evening and see how he had changed, even in that short time. The reading stated, " . . . note the difference in what you are thinking and what you are thinking about, what your desires are, what your experiences are!" (830-3)

In another case history from the Cayce files, a sixty-six-year-old woman obtained a reading to explore the past-life connections she had with people in her life. In addition to providing the past-life associations, the reading advised her that one of her greatest challenges was practicing and applying the attitudes, ideas, and high-mindedness that were already a part of her nature. She was encouraged to find a balanced approach in this application by doing things for herself as well as for others: "For he that contributes only to his own welfare soon finds little to work for. He that contributes only to the welfare of others soon finds too much of others and has lost the appreciation of self, or of its ideals." (3478-2)

A thirty-five-year-old man who sought mental and spiritual guidance was encouraged to do what he knew to do that would enable those patterns and shortcomings out of keeping with spiritual wholeness to simply fall by the wayside. The reading reminded him, "What is karma but giving away to impulse? Just as has been experienced by this entity, when the entity has sung Hallelujah it was much harder to say 'dammit.'" (622-6) He was encouraged to begin minimizing the faults he saw in others and magnifying their virtues. He would know he had been successful in his own soul development when the time came that he could see beauty, good, and godliness even in someone he had once hated.

Perhaps one of the most important (and often overlooked) elements enabling people to change and transform themselves is consistency of application. In a contemporary example, Norrene says that the most challenging experience in her life involved her ex-husband. Married and with a four-year-old son, the couple began to travel very different paths when the husband became an avid member of an extreme fundamentalist church. At the time, Norrene had an interest in metaphysics, comparative religious studies, and meditation. In addition to giving all of their savings to the church on the advice of the church's nineteen-year-old pastor, Norrene's husband filed court papers against her saying that she was an unfit mother and demanding custody of their child. In her husband's mind, she was filled with the devil and was a negative influence on their son, "because I had books on yoga, Cayce, and Buddhism." In addition to ending their marriage, her husband's new religious beliefs completely tore their son apart. The child was filled with horror stories about his mother's activities, giving him nightmares. In time, the couple's divorce was final, and Norrene got custody.

Since she respected her son's right to have contact with his father, she was patient and silent about how she felt about her ex-husband, "but it was very difficult to send my son up to his father's for the summer and have him come back a Bible-thumping 'saved' seven year old who told me I wasn't a good Christian because I didn't spank him." She resolved to continue applying her beliefs, assisting her son however she could and trying not to confuse him with conflicting ideas.

In her own words, Norrene "lived out her spirituality" through consistent application, meditation, and attunement and "simply paid attention to the best mom I could be." The problem went on for years, but Norrene continued her approach. Finally, her persistence paid off. Today, her son still maintains a good relationship with his father, and her ex-husband's antagonism toward her and her beliefs is no longer an issue.

In the Cayce cosmology, the keys to soul development include setting ideals, working with attunement, and consistent application. Setting an ideal simply involves choosing a motivation against which you can measure your attitudes and actions and then moving beyond habit patterns that are out of alignment with the best that you have to offer the world. Personal attunement is the process of awakening the self to a higher level of consciousness, a greater reality that recognizes the oneness of all creation and each individual's connection to that Source. Consistent application of anything enables that idea, principle, or skill to move beyond the level of mere knowledge and ideas to a much greater position of mastery and personal awareness. Application is also the tool that enables each person to move beyond where they are right now to where they are ultimately destined to be.

What if spiritual growth were not just an interesting idea but an inevitable process for everyone? What if the destiny of every soul were to conform to a pattern of love and wholeness? What if we were called not only to transform ourselves but also to act as channels of light and love to the world as a whole? What if personal transformation and growth enabled us to become who we really are? What if, ultimately, soul development were simply the process of spiritual attunement and personal application?

A Selection of Affirmations
from the Edgar Cayce Readings

These affirmations are included for contemplation and/
or for meditation and personal attunement.

Affirmation One:
Not my will but Thine, O Lord, be done in and through
me. Let me ever be a channel of blessings, today, now, to
those that I contact, in every way. Let my going in, mine
coming out be in accord with that Thou would have me
do, and as the call comes, "Here am I, send me, use me!"
262-3

Affirmation Two:
Our Father and our God! Here am I. Use Thou me as
Thou hast seen, as Thou seest best. Let me in every way
be a channel of blessings to others today. 3250-1

Affirmation Three:
Lord, help Thou me to fulfill the mission Thou hast for
me in the earth at this time. Let my thoughts, my activities, my purposes, be wholly in keeping with that Thou
would have me do. 1688-8

Affirmation Four:
Let thy patience, thy tolerance, thy activity be of such a
positive nature that it *fits* thee—as a glove—to be patient
with thy fellow man, to minister to those that are sick, to
those that are afflicted, to sit with those that are shut-in,
to read with those that are losing their perception, to reason with those that are wary of the turmoils; showing
brotherly love, patience, persistence in the Lord, and the
love that overcometh all things.

These be the things one must do. And do find patience
with self. 518-2

Affirmation Five:
Let that light be within me in such measures that I, as a child of God, may realize His love for man. May I live that, then, in my life day by day. 262-129

Affirmation Six:
Thy will, O Lord, be done in and through me as Thou seest I have need of for my soul development, and that I may through this development be the greater channel of blessing to my fellow man. 288-37

Affirmation Seven:
Then know that while the life is in a changing world, with changing friendships, changing environs and changes of every nature—unless there is accomplished that which lives on and *on* in the heart and soul, little has been or may be accomplished by self in its dealings with its fellow man.

Be acquainted, then, with that home beyond. Take time not merely to be holy or good, but good for something—good in that ye bring each day some new hope, some new opportunity, some new experience in the life of someone—a boy, a child, a babe, an old person who has lost the way in one manner or another. Thus ye will gradually build those steps which may carry you beyond the vale of those who see only the material blessings. For ye will know of Whom, in Whom ye have heard that "His words passeth not away."

So, though changes come, though the heavens may be in turmoil, though the earth and all the activities may be in riot, thy deeds done in such a way and manner will not change but live in the heart and the mind in such a manner as to bring that peace and harmony which comes only to those who take thought of just being kind to the other fellow! 1723-1

Affirmation Eight:

May that strength as was manifest in the consciousness of the Christ life be so magnified in me as to make every atom of my body conscious of His presence working in and through me, bringing that to pass as He sees I have need of now. 281-12

Affirmation Nine:

Open Thou mine eyes, O God, that I may know the glory Thou hast prepared for me. 262-89

Affirmation Ten:

Create in me, O God, a new purpose, a righteous spirit: that I may, as Thy child, be a living example of that I have professed and do profess to believe, by manifesting same among my fellow men. 262-124

Affirmation Eleven:

Let there be performed in my body that service, that activity O Father, Thou seest necessary to make my body whole; that I may be the greater service for Thee in this experience. 560-6

Affirmation Twelve:

Let the knowledge of the Lord so permeate my being that there is less and less of self, more and more of God, in my dealings with my fellow man; that the Christ may be in all, through all, in His name. 262-95

Affirmation Thirteen:

Lord, here am I! Use me, in the manner and the way Thou seest that I may best manifest Thee in the earth! Let my going in, my coming out, be acceptable in Thy sight day by day. And may I ever live, act, think, that what I do and say will be in keeping with Thy will. 361-11

Affirmation Fourteen:
Our Father, who art in heaven, may Thy kingdom come in earth through Thy presence in me, that the light of Thy word may shine unto those that I meet day by day. May Thy presence in my brother be such that I may glorify Thee. May I so conduct my own life that others may know Thy presence abides with me, and thus glorify Thee. 262-30

Affirmation Fifteen:
Father, God! Let me, as Thy child, see in my fellow man the divinity I would worship in Thee. 262-130

Affirmation Sixteen:
Lord, I am Thine, wholly—in body, in mind, in purpose. Be Thou the guide, O God, in my daily problems, my daily going ins and coming outs. 303-24

Affirmation Seventeen:
Lord, let that which is best for me—that I may be of the greater service—be my purpose, my hope, and my activity now. 2803-4

Affirmation Eighteen:
Lord, use me in the service of my country, in the service of my fellow man, in such a way and manner that I may do so to Thy name and glory. And may it bring that awareness, that consciousness of the closer walk with the Christ. 361-15

Affirmation Nineteen:
Into Thy hands, O Father, I give myself; in body, in mind; that Thy forces of good, Thy influence, may be manifested to those I contact day by day. 379-12

Affirmation Twenty:

Know that if you would be forgiven, if you would have friends, if you would know peace you must *make* friends, be kind, be joyous, be *content*—but *never* satisfied! For that longing which arises to better thyself is not merely that thy body may take ease, or that ye may gratify the appetites thereof! but it is rather that glory of the hope within for the greater knowledge of the spiritual life to *grow* and *bloom* in thy workaday life. 1723-1

Affirmation Twenty-One:

Father, God! Create in my mind, my body, that purpose that Thou would have; that there may be the demonstration, the manifestation of Thy spirit, of Thy purpose with Thy servant.

Let my body, my mind, be such as to keep attuned to the best that may come as a channel of blessings to others. 1523-7

Affirmation Twenty-Two:

Let my desire and my needs be in Thy hands, Thou Maker, Creator of the universe and all the forces and powers therein! And may I conform my attitude, my purpose, my desire, to that Thou hast as an activity for me. 462-8

Affirmation Twenty-Three:

There is being carried into my physical body that which will aid in enlivening tissue, that I may exercise the faculties of my body the better. This being carried through creative forces as are from God's storehouse. 5532-2

Affirmation Twenty-Four:

Let the body, the mind, be so in accord with the Divine, that may find expression through me, that there may come into my experience and my associations with my fellow man that which is in keeping with that purpose Thou, O Lord, hast for me to do! 555-11

Affirmation Twenty-Five:
I am Thine, O Lord! In Thee do I put my trust. Open Thou my understanding that I may receive, consciously, that Thou would have me do from day to day. Let me be a channel of blessing to someone each day. Let me be and so live that I may constrain others to glorify Thee. 620-3

Affirmation Twenty-Six:
Here am I, Lord, seeking to be a channel of help and blessings to others. Use Thou me in the way and manner Thou seest fit. I acknowledge my weaknesses, but I look for the promised strength in Thee to keep me in the way I should go. 1467-11

Affirmation Twenty-Seven:
Let others do as they may but for thee and thy house, love a living God. Keep His precepts. Thou knowest the way and that it is good. Then seek and ye shall find, knock and it shall be opened unto thee day by day. For others look to thee oft for counsel. When ye least suspect ye are an example for others. 262-109

Affirmation Twenty-Eight:
Lord, here am I. Use Thou me in that way and manner that I may be a better channel of service to Thee, and for bringing grace and mercy to those I meet day by day. 2051-5

Affirmation Twenty-Nine:
Our Father, our God! Hear Thy servant, as I seek to do Thy biddings. Create in me a pure heart. Search me, O God, and make me in that attitude, that activity, that is in keeping with Thy purpose with me now. 379-19

Affirmation Thirty:
Keep thy heart singing, for there is music and joy in the Happiness of knowing that you may be—and are—at a oneness with Him. Though there may come disturbances, shadows, turmoils, these must pass in the light of patience, persistence, lovingkindness. 262-109

Affirmation Thirty-One:
As ye would that men should do to you, do ye even so to them. Let the fruits of the spirit be manifested in thy life day by day. Be not afraid to just be kind, just be patient, just be longsuffering even with those that would speak ill of thee. For what glory hast thou if thou dost good only to those that do good to thee? 835-1

8

Light
to a
Waiting
World

*. . . unless each soul entity (and this entity especially)
makes the world better, that corner or place of the world
a little better, a little bit more hopeful, a little bit more
patient, showing a little more of brotherly love, a little
more of kindness, a little more of longsuffering—by the
very words and deeds of the entity, the life is a failure . . .*
3420-1

What if all individuals shared a purpose and reason for
which they had decided, as souls, to come into the earth?
What if that essential purpose in any given incarnation
were simply to become a better channel of the Creator's
love, light, and activity? What if—as co-workers with
God—we were endowed with the responsibility of transforming the earth into a place of peace, an environment
of understanding and compassion, where all individu-

als could truly become whole and reawaken to their connection with one another? What if the dawn of a new age, the creation of a new world order, and the timing of an awakening to a new paradigm in which we understand the nature of ourselves and our relationship to the Whole were within our grasp?

From the perspective of the Edgar Cayce readings, each individual is ultimately a companion to and a cocreator with God. Although inevitable, this relationship is not forced but only comes to pass as each soul chooses to allow its occurrence. We have the free will to postpone the inevitable, but not to change it. In our limited awareness, we often forget that what we truly want is what our soul has wanted all along. In a very real sense, the Creator's fondest desire is to experience companionship with each soul, thus finding expression in the earth through us, the children of an all-loving God.

With this in mind, Cayce often told people that they had the potential to make the world a better place by being used as channels for spiritual activity in the earth. Regardless of one's station in life or one's perception of worthiness, each person has the ability to make a major contribution in this direction. Whenever individuals are willing, setting their personal interests aside and choosing instead to be open to allowing God's will to work through them, incredible things might begin to transpire. Illustrating this very point is one of the most fascinating historical examples from the readings, that of U.S. president Woodrow Wilson (1856-1924).

As background information, Woodrow Wilson held only one political office before becoming president (1913-1921). Educated at the University of Virginia and Johns Hopkins University, he served in various teaching positions before receiving a professorship at the College of New Jersey (Princeton University). He was a professor for twelve years before becoming president of Princeton in 1902. Because of his writing, teaching, and speaking skills, he became one of the foremost academic personalities in the country. As a result of his prominence, in 1910 he was offered the Democratic nomination for governor of New Jersey, which he accepted. He won in a landslide victory and quickly established a name for himself as a progressive leader. Because of the many positive reforms he introduced as governor, he gained national attention and, in the 1912 presidential election, Wilson received the Democratic Party nomination and won the election, becoming the twenty-eighth president of the United States.

In retrospect, it may seem amazing that Woodrow Wilson served only a portion of one term in a political office before being nominated to the highest position in the country. However, the readings state that he held to an extremely high ideal, enabling him to be used as a channel of peace to humankind. In citing Wilson's life, Cayce acknowledged that the president would not even have been considered by most as a very religious man, but he was driven by more than his own interests, by hoping to help establish peace on earth. That choice had encouraged the activity of spirit to work through him, perhaps increasing the likelihood that he could rise from the position of university professor to president-elect of the United States in just ten years.

After World War I, President Wilson became convinced that world peace would become a reality only through international cooperation and the establishment of a League of Nations. More than any other president up to that time, Wilson was responsible for increasing the U.S. involvement in world affairs. His concept for the League was that countries would confront potential global problems through their united political and military strength. Wilson's idea gained international support, and the League of Nations came into reality as part of the

Treaty of Versailles, which put an end to the First World War. For his efforts, Woodrow Wilson was awarded the Nobel Peace Prize in 1919.

According to the Cayce readings, during Wilson's negotiations for the League, Spirit had actually sat with him, for there was an opportunity to establish an ideal upon which the entire world could agree. Forty-two nations took part in the first meeting of the League in Geneva in 1920. Eventually, sixty-three nations became members of the League of Nations at one time or another. Unfortunately, due to opposition party politics that defeated membership approval in the U.S. Senate, the United States never did become a member, striking a severe blow to Wilson's dream for global security and planetary peace. Wilson died in 1924, never seeing his dream come to a fuller realization through the establishment of the United Nations during World War II. The League eventually dissolved and transferred its assets to the United Nations.

Certainly a person does not have to be president to help transform the world. Cayce often told people that they were responsible only for their own lives and that corner of the world in which they found themselves. In this manner, the readings encouraged a forty-nine-year-old widow that all she need do was "*comfort* those that are heavyhearted, those that have lost their way mentally, those that have allowed stumblingblocks of grudges and of hate to build that which prevents them from awakening to the forces that lie within their inner selves." (1037-1) On other occasions, Cayce simply encouraged people "to become a light" to those who were in need.

The readings often reminded people that the Creator's desire is to work through every soul in the earth. With this in mind, when a small group of Edgar Cayce's supporters approached him about studying his work in depth, Cayce agreed and began to provide lessons in soul development that would enable each of them to "present a light to a waiting world." (262-2) In time, these lessons would have a major impact upon members of that small group as well as upon tens of thousands of others who have studied the material in the decades since.

The idea for the "Study Club," as those asking for the soul development readings originally called themselves, came about simply enough. At one time, a hospital dedicated to studying and working with Cayce's information on health operated in Virginia Beach. Unfortunately, funding was withdrawn during the Depression, and the hospital had to close in 1931. While it was open, however, lectures were offered to the public on Sunday afternoons. A small group from those gatherings wished to continue meeting even after the hospital was no longer in operation. Eventually, Florence Edmonds, one of the group members asked, "Mr. Cayce, couldn't we meet regularly as a group and study your work?"

Some members of the group hoped to become more spiritual. Others were interested in discovering how Cayce's amazing talent actually worked. Many hoped to become helpful to their families and even to the world at large. Years later, Cayce's secretary, Gladys Davis, reported that, in addition to these expectations, each member of that first group hoped to become more psychic in their own right. On September 14, 1931, seventeen people came together, and the group that would later call themselves Norfolk Study Group #1 had their first meeting.

Instead of receiving a discourse on psychic development, group members received the first in a series of lessons on spiritual growth that had to be applied in every area of their lives. The focus of Cayce's counsel was not on such things as yogic breathing, altered states of consciousness, or mind training but, instead, on such practical topics as *Cooperation, Virtue and Understanding, Patience, The Lord Thy God Is One,* and *Love.* Through the process of working with this material, members of the group learned to guard their thoughts and their words, establish spiritual ideals, and attempt to become better people in the process. In addition, they had to agree to undertake daily disciplines of meditation and prayer.

They were not provided with a series of simple and straightforward readings on spiritual knowledge and information. Rather, for the next eleven years, they committed themselves to lessons in soul development that had to be applied, understood, and lived before Cayce would give them the subject for the next lesson. The goal of their efforts was the practical application of spiritual principles in everyday life. The group's experiences with the first twelve lessons were eventually compiled into a manual for personal spiritual growth, entitled *A Search for God, Book I.* A second set of twelve lessons eventually followed, exploring a higher octave of principles similar to those in the first volume. In addition to undergoing personal growth and development, members of Norfolk Study Group #1 became extremely psychic. This interrelationship of the psychic to their studies was understandable to the group because the readings often insisted that psychic development was a result of soul growth.

In a similar vein, when a twenty-three-year-old electrical engineering student asked about developing his own psychic abilities, Edgar Cayce advised him that the best approach would be spiritual development through the process of setting ideals, attunement, and personal application (440-8). In Cayce's cosmology, although psychic experiences could be induced through mental exercises and the concentration of the mind, true psychic ability was a natural byproduct of soul development and spiritual growth.

Members of the first group were not outstanding students of metaphysics or budding psychics. They were housewives, secretaries, government employees, and teachers, but they did become psychic in the process of working with the Cayce material on soul development. Harmon Hartzell Bro, Ph.D. (1919-1997), psychotherapist, educator, and author, knew Edgar Cayce personally and witnessed more than five hundred readings. In time, he came to know and interview members of Norfolk Study Group #1 as well. In discussing some of his experiences with members of that group, he recalled:

I remember my astonishment when a middle-aged housewife from this group told me with striking accuracy the substance of a dream of mine which she had picked up psychically (she also went on to interpret the dream with considerable skill). And I remember my surprise when another member of this group spotted a vitamin deficiency in one of my children—about a week before our doctor did.

Healing, auras, vocational counsel, warnings, marital guidance, interpretation of symbols, seeing discarnates—all of these psychic phenomena and more are in my case notes on the members of "Group One." (*Fate,* March 1967)

Charles Thomas Cayce, grandson of Edgar Cayce and eldest son of Hugh Lynn Cayce, recalls an experience he had with Hannah Miller, a member of the first study group as well as a companion prayer group—an experience that confirmed the psychic abilities of the members of the group. During the 1950s, when he was still a young boy, he frequently rode his bicycle between where his father worked at the A.R.E. and his home fourteen blocks to the south. Over the summer and school breaks,

Charles Thomas often carried his father's lunch to the A.R.E. on his bicycle.

On one occasion, he arrived at the A.R.E. during some kind of lecture break to find approximately thirty people wandering around the lobby. The building was often full of people, including a couple of older women who had known his grandfather and who were often present at programs and activities. Young Charles Thomas went out of his way to avoid one of these women in particular, Hannah Miller, since she seemed to delight in giving him massive hugs in the grip of her large frame, while also planting a big kiss on his cheek. This whole interaction and display of affection were quite embarrassing to the young man.

In order to avoid the crowd, Charles Thomas went around the A.R.E. headquarters in order to sneak in the back way to his father's office. As he remembers it:

> I was excited to see my dad because I planned to tell him something that I hadn't told anybody. Earlier that day I had caught a big fish and, although it had gotten away, it had been quite a memorable experience and I wanted to tell him about it. No sooner had I arrived in the back door than there was Hannah Miller. She smiled at me and before I could duck away, she leaned over and gave me a big hug and a kiss on the cheek. Before leaving me, however, she whispered in my ear: "That was some fish you caught today."

Even now, he clearly remembers his response: "Her words nearly knocked my socks off! I couldn't believe it was possible. That experience really jolted me! It brought to mind the fact that my father had often mentioned how sensitive some of the individuals in that first study group really became."

On another occasion, group member Florence Edmonds had gone to the hospital to visit an acquaintance because, during one of her meditations, a voice had told her to go and pray for that individual. In spite of having to care for a family member of her own who was also sick at the time, Florence followed the instructions, went to the hospital, and sat next to a woman named Helen, the acquaintance's mother, just as the woman was being taken into the operating room. Later, as she was praying, Florence appeared startled, looked up, and told Helen, "We almost lost her." After the operation was over, the doctor came out and told Helen that her daughter had nearly died on the operating table: "We almost lost her," he said, echoing Florence's words. Peritonitis had set in, and surgery had been performed just in time (263-9 Reports).

Members of Norfolk Study Group #1 also had innumerable psychic experiences, including perceiving other people's akashic records, seeing visions, encountering personal healing experiences, having past-life dreams, communicating with deceased loved ones, and experiencing symbolic visions of their own soul's progress. Years later, in discussing the most helpful aspects of intuition and sensitivity that become available to those who undertake a commitment to soul development, Hugh Lynn Cayce (1907-1982) mentioned heightened communication, creativity, and the ability to work with healing:

> The real kind of telepathy is not the phenomenon of reading a mind or picking up on an emotion, but the capacity to sense the needs of another human being. It is a sensitivity of knowing when to praise, when to encourage, when to listen to an individual, when to pray for an individual. It relates first perhaps to those who are closest to us, to those we love

the most, by being able to comprehend the needs and the real attitudes of another human being whom we love and with whom we frequently fail to communicate in any meaningful manner. This kind of telepathy, a new awareness on a different level than just words, can be a very enriching experience for all concerned.

Second, what about the ability of *stirring creativity?* There certainly seems to be a great deal of relationship between psychically gifted people and creativeness . . . as one becomes more psychic, or more sensitive, there should be an expression and a move to become more creative in daily thought, in words, and in acts.

Third, *healing* is a natural part of growth of psychic sensitivity. It may start with the simple prayers for one's family or for other members of the group. Healing at physical, emotional, mental, and spiritual levels takes place now and then. From this point it can move on to greater sensitivity in which, by touching an individual, one can become a channel for healing. We touch people with our minds, with our words, and with our bodies. I have always sensed that we are at all times healers or destroyers. There is no middle ground. (A.R.E., 1980)

From Edgar Cayce's perspective, psychic experiences are simply the result of spiritual growth and attunement and not an end unto themselves. The purpose of life is to become a better channel through which the Creator can manifest in the earth, not to have a vision or some lofty spiritual experience. This ability to become a light to others and a channel through which God can operate in the material world is the rationale behind the lessons in soul development given to the first group. Those lessons were not to be limited to Norfolk Study Group #1, however.

Instead, Edgar Cayce predicted that the spiritual lessons given to that group would still be available for exploration and study by the rest of the world a hundred years later (262-71). Today, from such humble beginnings, these lessons in spiritual growth have expanded to include hundreds of study groups around the globe, foreign translations, and a variety of resource materials.[4]
The twelve lessons outlined for the first group are:

1. *Cooperation:* From Cayce's perspective, cooperation is not simply trying to work with another person; rather, it is a state of being that sets aside personal agendas, enabling God to use an individual as a "channel of blessings" to someone else.

2. *Know Thyself:* Rather than identification only with the physical life and *personality self,* the emphasis is on the true spiritual nature of the soul and the necessity of calling forth from within oneself the godlike qualities that are the essence of the *individuality self.*

3. *What Is My Ideal?* An ideal is the basic rationale behind an individual's actions; ultimately it is the *why* that motivates one's entire being. For that reason, the lesson's emphasis is on selecting a spiritual ideal that can begin to direct and shape the course of one's life in a positive direction.

4. *Faith:* Cayce related true faith to an attitude of open trust. It is *not* belief, dogma, or religion; instead, it is an awareness that allows the energy of

---

[4]In addition to the original readings given to Norfolk Study Group #1 (the 262 series), supplemental materials include the *Search for God* books and companion resources, such as *Your Life: Why It Is the Way It Is and What You Can Do About It* (MacArthur), *Twelve Lessons in Personal Spirituality* (Todeschi), etc.

Spirit to work through individuals in spite of their shortcomings and imperfections.

5. ***Virtue and Understanding:*** Virtue is essentially living up to the best that an individual knows to do; understanding is knowledge that has been applied.

6. ***Fellowship:*** The readings suggest that fellowship is about creating community. It is about minimizing another's faults and magnifying another's strengths. It is about growing in the realization of our connection with one another and our shared connection to God.

7. ***Patience:*** In the Cayce information, patience is not about passiveness or submission. Patience is about becoming consciously aware of self and all impelling influences in a situation, then striving to offer the best one has to offer in return. Patience is actually an activity of the body, mind, and soul, focused in such as way as to allow God's love, laws, and presence to come into our lives.

8. ***The Open Door:*** Beyond the personality self, there is a pattern of perfection within each soul that can be manifested in that person's life through right thought and right action. The ultimate expression of one's true individuality is waiting to be awakened by the human will.

9. ***In His Presence:*** Even though we are always in God's presence, we forget to open ourselves to the awareness that He is always in ours. Our ultimate destiny is to come to the realization of our true relationship with the Creator.

10. ***The Cross and the Crown:*** Considered by some to be one of the most challenging in the series, this lesson explores the purpose of reincarnation and why the soul must "meet self" in order to overcome the "crosses" (or habit patterns or desires) that stand between the person and a full awareness of

one's spiritual nature. The "crown" is the ultimate awareness of our destiny and our heritage as children of a loving God.

11. ***The Lord Thy God Is One:*** The readings contend that there is only *one force* in the universe and that Force is God. Although humankind can misuse this One Force of Spirit that underlies all of creation, and create evil in the process, ultimately everything must be brought in alignment to the universality of that One Force. In other words, there is but one God, and we are all His children.

12. ***Love:*** Love is the best expression of that one universal Force. True love reaches out to others without regard for what is received in return. In a very real sense, from Cayce's perspective, the primary purpose of life is to let the love of God flow through us.

Taken together, these lessons offer people from all walks of life and religious backgrounds a practical approach to personal transformation and spiritual development. In Cayce's cosmology, although our collective destiny is one of wholeness, this future becomes inevitable only as we bring it to fruition in our own lives. In other words, the journey upon which we are traveling has got to include elements of our ultimate destination, or else we are never going to get there. Until we are willing and able to incorporate the elements of a new age of peace and love for all of humankind into our own lives and our surroundings, this utopian ideal of a new world will remain beyond reach. For that reason, each of us is challenged to become "a light to a waiting world."

Unlike a merely philosophical idea, it is possible to bring elements of this new world into our lives each and every day. Simply stated, whatever is out of alignment with the world we hope to create needs to be changed. If we hope to have peace, then we need to resolve any conflict that remains in our own lives. In a practical sense, we can't harbor animosity, resentment, or even weapons of destruction if we hope to create peace. If we long for a beautiful and supportive planet that inspires and nurtures its inhabitants, we cannot allow ourselves to be fascinated by end-of-the-world prophecies, earth-change maps, or fears that blind us to the beauty of creation that is already about us. If our desire is to create a world of hope, attitudes of love, and lives filled with compassion, then we need to cultivate each of these elements in all of our relationships right now.

In discussing possibilities for this kind of a future, individuals too often respond with, "Yes, that kind of a world would be wonderful *but . . .* " and then begin to assert all the reasons why such a world is not possible. What these individuals need to keep in mind is that although such a world may not be feasible for the Whole at this time, it is possible in their own lives even now. Although threats of war and global terrorism may prevent a country from achieving total disarmament, these planetary issues need not have an effect upon what an individual does in his or her own life. In the long run, as individuals change themselves and their interactions with one another, eventually the world cannot help but follow.

The Edgar Cayce readings foresaw the Aquarian Age as a time when humankind would finally begin to become serious about the purpose of life and the nature of the soul. It is destined to be a time when all individuals realize their connection and responsibility to all others. It will be an age when God's influence will be acknowledged and consciously experienced in everyday life. It is to be an era when the Creator will communicate directly with His children and they, in turn, will be fully conscious of that interaction. From Cayce's perspective, it is to be a glorious time when heaven itself has the ability to come into the earth. However, it is not a time that will manifest suddenly, so that one day we wake up and it has arrived. Instead, it is a world that must be built "line upon line" by each individual daily. This transformation in consciousness will be so subtle that Cayce told a forty-one-year-old housewife in 1939 that "*only* those who accept same will even become aware of what's going on about them!" (1602-3) Let each of us—as potential lights to one another—hope to be among that number.

What if a new understanding of the nature of the soul and the purpose of life on earth could transform the planet? What if this understanding were brought about not through dogma or belief, but through the practical application of spiritual principles in everyday life? What if we are individually responsible for our personal and global futures? What if the current conditions existing in the world today are simply the reflection of what we have and have not done to bring the reality of Spirit into the earth? What if, truly, we are light to a waiting world?

Conclusion

Then, the Destiny of the Soul—as of all creation—is to be one with Him; continually growing, growing, for that association. 262-88

(Q) Anything else that may be given at this time?
(A) Anything else?!! Worlds! *Worlds might be filled with that as might be given!* 2156-2

Perhaps now, more than ever before, humankind is in need of a worldview shift. Collectively, we must change our perceptions of what life is all about. The condition of the planet makes it clear that life cannot be about differences or animosities. It is not about fear or lack. It is not about possessions or power. It is not about abuse or victimization. It is simply about the process of personal transformation and development, leading to the next step in our collective growth and awakening awareness. In answer to age-old questions—"Who am I?" "Why am I here?" and "What is the purpose of life?"—the new world paradigm ultimately suggests that we are made in the image of God, we are destined to conform to that image, and life is about learning this simple truth.

To this end, our spiritual growth is not dependent upon who or what we are or even what happens to us; rather, it is connected to how we deal with the people and events that come into our lives. Ultimately, everything has the potential to be a helpful, learning experience in our own awakening and development if we only choose to make it so. Life's lessons are brought to us as a means of overcoming flaws and weaknesses as well as cultivating and applying soul qualities and strengths. Each of those weaknesses is simply an indication of the personality's selfishness that has yet to be overcome, while one's strengths are the manifestation of the individuality's selfless love. In Cayce's cosmology, the primary purpose of soul development is to reestablish a conscious awareness of our spiritual nature and our oneness with God. This state of enlightenment becomes ours simply by learning and applying the lessons of unconditional love or by literally attaining perfection in the earth. One way or another, this is the destiny of every soul.

It stands to reason that, if the goal of each individual in the process of growth toward soul perfection is to begin to manifest the qualities of the Creator, then from time to time in history, we would inevitably see examples of God's activity in the earth. For this reason, the new paradigm will be extremely challenging to traditional religion. It suggests that, for thousands of years, much of the world has misunderstood the life of every religious leader. Whether the leader was Jesus, Buddha, Muhammad, Moses, Zoroaster, or Krishna, the new paradigm maintains that they called the world not to follow them as a god but to follow their example *so that we could become more godlike,* just as they did.

Since the example most often cited in the Edgar Cayce readings is Jesus, let us delve further into His life, looking at this very possibility. Unfortunately, because of the present usage of the terms *Jesus* and *Christian,* many have become embarrassed about even mentioning the words. Often, people would rather acknowledge their interest in almost any other religious group than to be identified with the contemporary descriptions of what it is claimed Jesus was all about. The problem is that much of what is said about Jesus was never a part of His ministry or His teachings. The new paradigm suggests that the Aquarian Age will reclaim Jesus as an elder brother, in spite of what the last two thousand years have done to Him.

Because of the abuses of the past, when people hear the terms *Christ* or *Jesus,* right away they may fall into preconceived notions based upon their upbringing or particular religious background. Throughout history, the perspectives people have had on the life and teachings of Jesus have been varied, often even at odds. Sometimes those involved in new age philosophies or comparative religious studies decide that Jesus was "just a teacher" or "only a prophet." Others have decided to disregard Him altogether. Members of non-Christian faiths may ignore His life and ministry. Was He a man who committed blasphemy by thinking Himself a god? Others have said, "Well, Christians have been cruel to me, and therefore I'm not interested in Jesus." Even among those who call themselves Christian, there is not complete agreement about the meaning of Jesus' life and work. These disagreements have resulted in dozens of denominational factions, charges of heresy or breaking away from the faith, and countless wars. The Edgar Cayce material, however, offers an approach that suggests there is a way of looking at the life of Jesus in a manner that unifies all of humankind rather than dividing it.

Cayce called Jesus our "elder brother" who can sometimes provide insight and counsel into some of life's difficulties—just as an older sibling can—because He went through them first. What may surprise us is that this fact has nothing to do with religion; it has to do with the true nature of our spirituality and discovering our relationship with God—a relationship we share with Jesus. The readings not only affirm that Jesus was a Son of God, but they also state the same thing about each and every one of us. In other words: *Jesus was like each one of us and, ultimately, each one of us is destined to be like Him!*

Although some may be repelled at first by such a suggestion, evidence for this very premise is found in the Bible and the Cayce readings. When speaking of humankind, Jesus, himself, said, "They are not of the world, even as I am not of the world." (John 17:16). Surprisingly, perhaps, a Jewish businessman expressed this same conclusion in questions that he posed to Edgar Cayce:

> (Q) Jesus was made perfect, God came into His Own. We are men not yet perfect, God not yet equal to God. He represents our so-called future, the path to the Throne.
>
> (A) Correct. He is the path to the throne, in that we, man, must become as the One as directs the way.
>
> (Q) . . . Like us, Jesus was both God and Man until He became God alone.
>
> (A) Correct. 900-100

Confirming our deep and inextricable connection to the Creator, in 1937, Cayce told another person:

Know that as you do unto the least of your associates, your acquaintances, yes—your enemies, you
do unto yourself in your relationships with your
Maker.
Then so live that you may ever look *every* man in
the face and see the reflection of your God. For the
soul of every man is the image of thy Maker. 361-9

Before becoming offended by this incredible possibility, shouting out charges of heresy or believing the idea
to be the work of the devil, we need to look closely at the
life of Jesus. Not only will we find that He was charged
with blasphemy for the very same claim, but we will find
that He stated this truth for each and every one of us:

I and my Father are one. Then [they] took up
stones again to stone him. Jesus answered them,
Many good works have I shewed you from my Father; for which of those works do you stone me?
[They] answered him, saying, For a good work we
stone thee not; but for blasphemy; and because that
thou, being a man, makest thyself God. Jesus answered them, Is it not written in your law, I said, Ye
are gods? John 10:30-34

The law Jesus referred to is the Old Testament, specifically Psalm 82, which asserts that, not only are we God's
children, but we are also "gods" (to be sure, gods in the
making), as well. Although some may be offended by the
statement that everyone is a part of God, in recent years,
more and more people working with esoteric spiritual
traditions have come to that very conclusion. Unfortunately, those who accept this premise often have forgotten the appropriate attitude that should accompany it.
In reality, this claim is not so much true as a statement
about one's self. Instead, it is only true as we become

godlike toward one another. In discussing soul growth, Edgar Cayce reminded a fifty-five-year-old chiropractor that he was a child of God and, therefore, a spiritual being:

> Act like it! Don't act like ye think ye are a God! Ye may become such, but when ye do ye think not of thyself. For what is the pattern [demonstrated by Jesus]? He thought it not robbery to make Himself equal with God, but He acted like it in the earth. 4083-1

When Jesus said, "I am the way, the truth, and the life" (John 14:6), it was not a call to religious conversion, but rather an opportunity for us to realize that His life could serve as an example. Regardless of our religious backgrounds, the life of Jesus demonstrated a pattern of love and a method of living in the earth that can enable each of us to overcome our personal weaknesses, our shortcomings, and even our problems. In the language of the Cayce readings:

> For the Master, Jesus, even the Christ, is the pattern for every man in the earth, whether he be Gentile or Jew, Parthenian or Greek. For all have the pattern, whether they call on that name or not; but there is no other name given under heaven whereby men may be saved from themselves. 3528-1

On one occasion, a thirty-eight-year-old man, who wanted additional information on how he might better manifest his life's purpose, asked Edgar Cayce for clarification on the words *Jesus* and *Christ:*

> (Q) What is the meaning and significance of the words Jesus and Christ . . . ?

(A) Just as indicated. Jesus is the man—the activity, the mind, the relationships that He bore to others. Yea, He was mindful of friends, He was sociable, He was loving, He was kind, He was gentle. He grew faint, He grew weak—and yet gained that strength that He has promised, in becoming the Christ, by fulfilling and overcoming the world! Ye are made strong—in body, in mind, in soul and purpose—by that power in Christ. The *power*, then, is in the Christ. The *pattern* is in Jesus. 2533-7

Rather than falling back onto old religious ideas or dogma, it is important to remember that the Christ Consciousness or God Consciousness or perfection consciousness has nothing to do with a specific religious group. Instead, this consciousness was simply described as "the awareness within each soul, imprinted in pattern on the mind and waiting to be awakened by the will, of the soul's oneness with God . . . " (5749-14)

The transformative power of this consciousness is awakened as individuals work at their own soul development. In fact, this awakening consciousness is the essential purpose for which each soul enters into life. When a thirty-six-year-old schoolteacher asked about the main purpose for her present incarnation, Cayce replied, "To glorify the Christ-Consciousness in the earth—in the lives of those with whom ye come in contact, and to live the same thyself." (2441-4) In terms of how this awareness would unfold in an individual's life, one person was told:

Not in mighty deeds of valor, not in the exaltation of thy knowledge or thy power; but in the gentleness of the things of the spirit: Love, kindness, longsuffering, patience; these thy brother hath shown thee that thou, applying them in thy associations with thy fellow man day by day, here a little, there a little, may become one with Him as He has *destined* that thou shouldst be! 849-11

In Cayce's cosmology, the new paradigm suggests that Jesus is an elder brother for all of humankind. This Jesus is not interested in religious conversion, denomination-alism, or even mighty personal accomplishments. Instead, He is simply interested in how we treat one another. With this in mind, even in the midst of our diversity as a human family, we share a common spiritual heritage. We are all children of the same God. We are all part of the one spiritual Source. We are all destined to return to our Creator, our Mother/Father, our God.

In addition to understanding the nature of each individual and our connection to one another, the new worldview will make it clear that life is not random and unfair; instead, it is purposefully orchestrated for the well-being of every single soul. It will contend that somehow each of us is actively responsible for cocreating the substance of our lives, just as we are held accountable for all of our actions, for all of our words and for all of our thoughts. It will champion the fact that the Creator is not aligned with one religious movement over another or even one person over another, for it is inevitable that everyone will make it. It will assert that an all-loving, ever-merciful, and eternally supportive God has provided a means for each of His children to grow and live and become all that they were meant to be.

What if the answer to the question "Who am I?" were much more than we had ever even dared to imagine? What if we were connected to and responsible for one another? What if there were no reason for prejudice or injustice because ultimately we are all the same? What if the awareness of what life is all about became the primary motivator for each and every soul? What if God loves each of us equally and has destined that we are to become like Him?

What if all of this were simply a matter of fact? What then? ◈

Made in the USA
Columbia, SC
23 January 2021

31438681R00114